Colette's Christmas

Colette's Christmas

COLETTE PETERS

Photographs by Alex McLean

LITTLE, BROWN AND COMPANY

BOSTON   NEW YORK   LONDON

Originally published in hardcover by Little, Brown and Company, 1993
First paperback edition, 1999

Library of Congress Cataloging-in-Publication Data

Peters, Colette.
　[Christmas]
　Colette's Christmas / Colette Peters: photographs by Alex McLean.
— 1st ed.
　　p.　　cm.
　Includes index.
　ISBN 0-316-70206-4 (hc) / 0-316-702765-5 (pb)
　1. Christmas cookery.　2. Confectionery.　I. Title.　II. Title:
Christmas.
　TX739.2.C45P48　　1993
641.5'66 — dc20　　　　　　　　　　　　　　　　　92-45279

10　9　8　7　6　5　4　3　2　1

IP

Printed in Hong Kong

To Mom and Dad, Danny, Doreen, Pat, and Jack —
for teaching me the true meaning of Christmas

Contents

Acknowledgments

I would like to sincerely thank the following people for their help in creating this book:

Mom, for helping me to develop and test recipes between Chicago and New York;

Chippy Irvine, for your generosity, kindness, and delicious meals;

Alex McLean, for your beautiful photographs;

Jennifer Josephy, for being so patient;

Angela Miller, for letting me cover your floors with dragées;

Margot Abel, for all those long nights of editing;

Karen Tack, for your culinary expertise and answers to so many questions;

Carol Baker, for all of your ornaments;

Linda Lieff, for your speedy answers to my pleas;

Terry, for finding those cookie cutters;

Kathy O'Connor, for helping me to organize;

Offray Ribbon Company;

Steve, for putting up with Christmas all summer long;

Laura Smith, for your constant, good-natured help.

Author's Note

CHRISTMAS has always been my favorite time of year. As a child I used to love helping my mom prepare for the big day. I would spend hours baking in the kitchen, creating pretty ornaments, and stringing popcorn to hang on the tree. I still love the weeks of shopping and wrapping gifts to bring home when I visit my family for the holidays. I especially like to bake cookies, cakes, and pies for the family festivities. And since I started my baking business, gingerbread houses have also become part of my Christmas repertoire.

The holiday season seems to bring out the child in everyone. People turn their creativity to making things that they wouldn't dream of attempting at any other time of year. By sharing my own ideas in this book, I hope to inspire your inventiveness and help to make your Christmas celebrations as festive as your imagination allows.

Before you begin, turn to the glossary of tools on pages 152–153 for a guide to the supplies needed to make the projects in this book. You may already have some of the equipment in your kitchen. The recipe sections contain all of the actual ingredients needed for the various projects. Most of these items can be found in the grocery store, but some can only be purchased in specialty stores, so plan ahead.

Each chapter progresses from simple projects to the more elaborate, so feel free to choose according to your level of confidence and patience.

Colette

Cookies

Many people make cookies for Christmas, even those who don't normally bake. And decorating them is a great way to involve the children in the holiday fun. They're a Christmas tradition to have when people drop in unexpectedly, or to nibble on between the main meal and the leftovers.

Penny Cookies

FOR AS LONG as I can remember, my mother has made these delicious cookies for Christmas. Now I make them for the holidays, too. They are wonderful as a simple rolled cookie, but they can also be used for cutout cookies. Adding cocoa to half of the dough turns them into delicious chocolate pinwheels.

Makes 4 dozen cookies

½ pound (2 sticks) softened butter or margarine
⅓ cup sugar
2⅛ cups flour
1 teaspoon vanilla extract
2 tablespoons unsweetened cocoa (optional)
variety of Christmas cookie cutters
colored sugar (can be store-bought, or you can make your own by adding a few drops of liquid food coloring to ½ cup of sugar, then stirring until all of the color is incorporated into the sugar)
wax paper
rolling pin
1 recipe royal icing (page 145)
pastry bags and couplers
tip #2
sharp knife
gold or silver dragées
edible glitter
sprinkles
colored candies
clear piping gel (available at cake-decorating stores)
small paintbrush

In a heavy-duty mixer, beat the butter until fluffy. Add the sugar, and beat together until well blended. Slowly add the flour, a few tablespoons at a time, while mixing at low speed. If you do not have a heavy-duty mixer, the last of the flour can be kneaded in by hand. Add the vanilla.

The dough needs to be chilled before baking. If you plan to make cutout cookies, place the dough in a large plastic bag and let it chill for a few hours.

To make simple rolled cookies, divide the dough into 2 equal sections and make 2 long rolls, about 1½ inches in diameter. Place each roll on a sheet of wax paper a little longer than the roll.

Sprinkle with colored sugar and roll the dough until it is covered with sugar. Wrap the dough in the paper and refrigerate for a few hours. When ready to bake, preheat the oven to 350 degrees F. Slice the dough into ¼-inch-thick cookies with a sharp knife and bake on a greased cookie sheet for 10 to 12 minutes or until golden brown.

To make pinwheel cookies, divide the dough into 2 equal parts and add 2 tablespoons unsweetened cocoa to half of the dough. Knead the cocoa into the dough until well blended. Place the plain dough on a piece of wax paper and flatten it slightly with your hands. Place another piece of wax paper on top of the dough and flatten it with a rolling pin to about ¼ inch thick. Repeat with the chocolate dough. Remove the top papers from both doughs, flip the chocolate dough on top of the plain dough, and flatten again, with a piece of wax paper on top, until the 2 layers combined are about ½ inch thick. Remove the top layer of wax

paper and roll the dough, jelly-roll style, into a long cylinder. Cover with colored sugar and refrigerate for a few hours. Cut and bake as for rolled cookies.

To make decorated cutout cookies, preheat the oven to 350 degrees F. Roll out the chilled dough to about ⅛ thick on a lightly floured surface. Cut out with cookie cutters, or use the patterns provided (patterns 1–4) and cut out the shapes with a sharp knife. Place the cookies on a greased cookie sheet and bake for 10 to 12 minutes or until golden brown. Cool the cookies on racks before decorating.

To decorate, make a recipe of royal icing and tint it to your desired colors. Keep the icing covered with a damp towel while you are working to prevent it from drying out. To cover a cookie with icing, thin some of the icing with a little water and spread it on the cookie with a knife or metal spatula. Leave some of the icing thick for piping borders or other designs, using the #2 tip. Add dragees, edible glitter, colored sprinkles, or other decorations to the wet icing. To attach candies to uniced cookies, brush a thin layer of clear piping gel on the cookie with a small paintbrush and add decorations.

Pattern 1

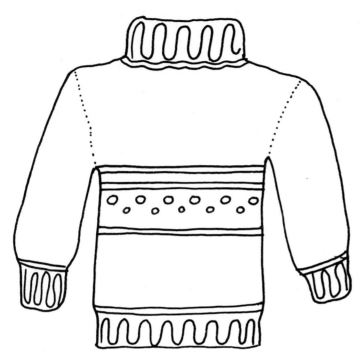

Pattern 2

Pattern 3

Pattern 4

Chow Mein Noodle Wreaths

*A*N UNUSUAL treat that is one of my favorites, this is really more of a candy than a cookie. I learned this recipe in third grade, when Nancy Segin taught us how to make them during show and tell. I've been making them for Christmas ever since. They're rich and delicious and even a child can make them — I guarantee it!

Makes 20 wreaths or 50 clusters

1 cup (6 ounces) semisweet chocolate chips
2 cups (12 ounces) Nestlé's butterscotch chips
1 cup cashews
1 large can (5 ounces) chow mein noodles
wax paper
small silver and gold dragées (optional)

Place the chocolate and butterscotch chips in the top of a double boiler or in a large saucepan on top of another pan filled halfway with water. Heat the water just to the boiling point, then turn off the heat. If the chocolate gets too hot, it will not melt correctly and will clump up into a hard mass. Stir the chips occasionally until they are completely melted and smooth. Remove the mixture from the heat and add the cashews and noodles. Stir with a large wooden spoon until all dry ingredients are coated.

To make wreaths, spoon the mixture in a wreath shape onto a sheet of wax paper placed on a cookie sheet. Sprinkle with dragées while the chocolate is still warm. Refrigerate until firm.

To make simple clusters, spoon a teaspoonful of the mixture onto a sheet of wax paper placed on a cookie sheet. Refrigerate until firm. These keep best if left refrigerated, but can also be stored in a cookie tin at room temperature, though they may become soft.

Mint Meringues

THESE LIGHT-AS-A-FEATHER cookies will melt in your mouth. A touch of mint makes them a refreshing treat after a heavy Christmas meal.

Makes 20 cookies

parchment or brown paper
2 egg whites, room temperature
⅛ teaspoon cream of tartar
¾ cup sugar
½ teaspoon mint extract
green liquid food coloring
pastry bag and coupler
tip #19
colored sprinkles or mini–chocolate chips for
    decorating

Preheat the oven to 275 degrees F. Place a sheet of parchment or brown paper on a cookie sheet. Beat the egg whites at medium speed until foamy. Add the cream of tartar. Beat at high speed until soft peaks form. Add the sugar one tablespoon at a time while beating. Continue beating on high until stiff peaks form. Fold in the mint extract and 2 or 3 drops of the food coloring, until the mixture is pale green. Place the meringue in a grease-free pastry bag with the #19 tip attached and pipe trees on the paper, using a widening zigzag motion. Sprinkle with mini–chocolate chips or colored sprinkles. Bake on the paper-covered cookie sheet for about 20 minutes or until dry *but not brown.*

Poinsettia Diamonds

CHRISTMAS would not be complete without poinsettias. The combination of oatmeal and chocolate makes this a delicious and festive cookie.

Makes 30 cookies

1 cup (2 sticks) softened butter or margarine
½ cup brown sugar, firmly packed
½ cup sugar
1 teaspoon vanilla extract
2 egg yolks, at room temperature
1 cup sifted flour
1 cup rolled oats
10 ounces milk or white chocolate
2 teaspoons butter
red-colored Fruit Roll-ups
small rose-petal cutter
green candied cherries
gold dragées

Preheat the oven to 325 degrees F. Cream the butter and the two sugars together. Beat in the vanilla and the egg yolks and continue beating on medium speed until fluffy. Add the flour and oats and mix thoroughly. Spread the mixture into a greased 9 × 13–inch pan. Bake for 20 minute or until golden brown. Meanwhile, melt the chocolate and the butter in a double boiler or over hot water. Let the cookies stand at room temperature for 10 minutes, then spread the chocolate mixture on top of the baked cookies. Cut into diamonds while still warm, as shown in figure 1.

To decorate the cookies, unroll a piece of the red Fruit Roll-ups and cut 6 petals with the rose cutter. Pinch the round end of the petal until it sticks together. Place the 6 petals with the pointed end facing out, in the center of each cookie, evenly spaced. Place a gold dragée in the center of

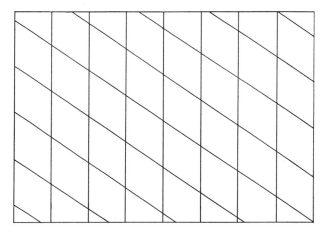

Figure 1

the flower. Cut out 2 small leaves from a candied cherry and place them on either side of the poinsettia.

Stocking Cookies

THESE COOKIES make great ornaments for the tree or mantel. They can be decorated in a variety of ways; I have shown just a few to give you some ideas. Have fun making them, and don't forget to let the kids join in.

Makes 6 cookies

2 recipes basic cookie or gingerbread-house dough (page 149 or 150)
cardboard
rolling pin
sharp knife
parchment paper (optional)
1 recipe royal icing (page 145)
pastry bags and couplers
tips #1, #2, #4, #48, and #67
red, green, blue, yellow, purple, and black paste food coloring
multicolored mini-jawbreakers, ¼ inch in diameter (found in bulk candy stores)
gold nontoxic powder
clear piping gel
gold dragées
ribbon or cord for hanging

Make the cookie dough according to the recipe. Preheat the oven to 350 degrees F. Enlarge the pattern shown (pattern 1) to 125 percent of its size, and trace it onto a piece of cardboard. Cut out the pattern. Roll out the cookie dough on a floured surface to about ¼ inch thick. Place the cardboard pattern on top of the dough and cut out with a sharp knife. Make a small hole about ¼ inch across in the top right-hand corner of the cookie for the ribbon (the hole should be no less than ½ inch from the edge of the cookie so that there will be enough strength to support its weight). Place the cutout dough on a greased or parchment-lined cookie sheet and bake about 12 minutes or until golden brown. Cool on wire racks until completely cool.

To decorate the cookies, see the directions that follow.

Holly Stocking

Tint about 2 tablespoons of royal icing blue, and thin it with a few drops of water. Spread over the cookie to cover, using a knife or metal spatula. Let the icing set for about 30 minutes.

Tint 3 tablespoons of the royal icing green. Using the #2 tip, pipe holly-leaf outlines, each about 1¼ inches long, spaced evenly around the surface of the cookie. Then thin the green icing with a few drops of water and fill in the holly leaves with the #1 tip.

Tint about ¼ cup of the royal icing red. Pipe the red holly berries with *slightly* thinned icing and the #2 tip. Let the cookie dry thoroughly, then insert a ribbon or cord, tie, and hang.

Christmas Tree Stocking

Spread the top of the cookie with about 2 tablespoons of thinned white royal icing. While the icing is still wet, place green mini-jawbreakers in a tree formation (an equilateral triangle with 1 candy as the trunk), using 16 candies to form each tree. The first tree should be centered about 1 inch from the top of the stocking. The next 2 trees should be about ¾ inch below and to the left and right of the top tree. Continue placing the rest of the trees in this formation. If the icing starts to dry before you are finished, pipe small dots of icing onto the back of each candy with the #1 tip. (*Hint:* It helps to use tweezers when handling these candies.)

Place multicolored jawbreakers with royal icing and the #1 tip around the trees. Pipe white dots between the colored candies, using slightly thinned royal icing and the #1 tip. Let the cookie dry completely, then insert the ribbon, tie, and hang.

As an alternative to using candies, you can use a #4 tip with slightly thinned, colored royal icing to make the trees and the multicolored dots.

Berry Stocking

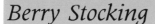

Tint 2 tablespoons of royal icing black and thin it with a few drops of water. Cover the cookie with the icing and let it dry for about 30 minutes.

Mark 1½-inch-wide diagonal stripes on the cookie with a toothpick and a ruler.

Mix 1/16 teaspoon of gold powder with 1 heaping tablespoon of clear piping gel. Using the #1 tip, pipe rows of lines in a herringbone formation with the gold gel along the marked lines, as shown in the photograph. Pipe gold outlines for the berries. Pipe gold dots around the perimeter of the cookie.

Tint about ¼ cup of the icing red and thin it with a few drops of water. Fill in the berry outlines with the red icing, using the #2 tip. Tint ¼ cup of the icing green. Use the #1 tip to pipe the stems and leaves of the berries with the green icing, using more pressure for the leaves. Pipe additional gold dots around the berries. Let the cookie dry, then insert a ribbon or cord in the hole, tie in a bow, and hang.

Striped Stocking

Tint 2 tablespoons of royal icing red and thin it with a few drops of water. Cover the cookie with the thinned icing and let it dry for about 30 minutes.

Starting at the top, pipe horizontal stripes across the stocking about ½ inch apart with white icing and the #48 tip. Follow the contour of the stocking, piping perpendicularly up to the foot of the stocking where it starts to curve.

Tint ½ cup of royal icing green. Using the #67 tip, pipe a horizontal green stripe between every other white stripe. This tip will automatically make a ruffled-edge stripe. While the green stripes are still wet, place five gold dragées evenly across each one.

Tint about ¼ cup of the royal icing pale purple. With tip #2, pipe a stripe of purple icing on each side of each white stripe. Let the cookie dry thoroughly, then insert a ribbon or cord, tie in a bow, and hang.

Teddy Bear

Bake the pattern pieces shown (patterns 1–5). Make 2 of the arm pieces. Glue the nose piece in the center of the bear's head with a dot of royal icing.

Thin 2 heaping tablespoons of royal icing with a few drops of water. Using a small paintbrush, brush the icing onto the bear's face above the nose, for the eyes. Tint the remaining thinned icing pink. Brush icing on the ears, hands, feet, and stomach, as shown in the photograph. Tint the remaining icing red and brush it on the nose. Let the icing dry completely.

When the icing is dry, brush the uniced areas of the bear with clear piping gel. Sprinkle small gold dragées over the gel. Tint a tablespoon of royal icing black. Pipe black dots in the center of the eyes and a black line for the mouth. When the gel is dry, attach the arms and legs to the body with red ribbon.

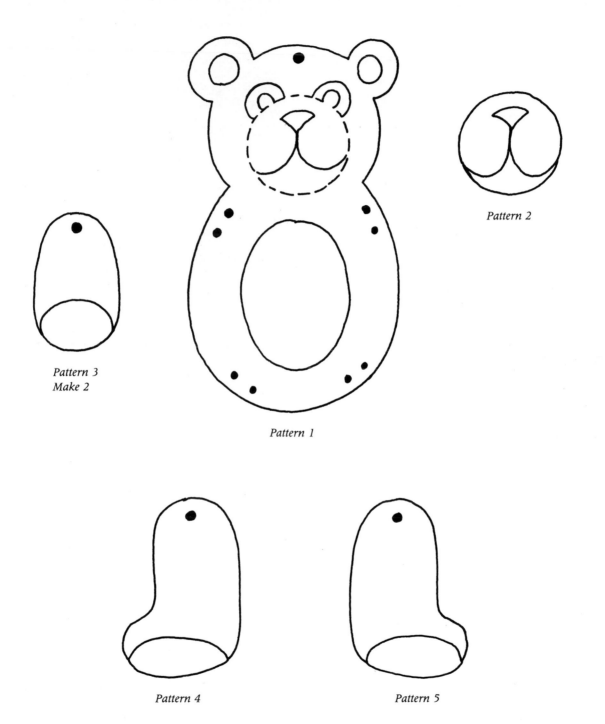

Pattern 2

Pattern 3
Make 2

Pattern 1

Pattern 4

Pattern 5

Santa Claus

Bake the pattern pieces shown (patterns 6–10). Thin 3 tablespoons of royal icing with a few drops of water. Tint the icing pink. Brush the icing on the face area, using a small paintbrush. Tint the remaining thinned icing red. Brush red icing on the cookies in the areas indicated in the photograph. Tint the remaining thinned icing black and brush on the pieces for the gloves, the boots, and the belt across Santa's middle. Set aside the remaining black icing, keeping it tightly covered so it will not dry out.

With the #2 tip and white unthinned royal icing, pipe curls for the fur cuffs on the arms between the black and red areas. Set aside the arms and legs to dry completely.

Pipe white fur on the coat, a beard, hair, eyebrows, a mustache, and fur on the cap. Pipe white dots for the eyes. Make sure to leave a space for Santa's nose and mouth.

Tint about a teaspoon of the white icing pink. Above the mustache, pipe a large dot of icing for the nose and 2 smaller dots on either side. Pipe a black dot in the center of each eye. Finally, to make the belt buckle, pipe a white square in the center of the belt and sprinkle yellow colored sugar over the wet icing.

Let all of the pieces dry completely before putting Santa together with red ribbon.

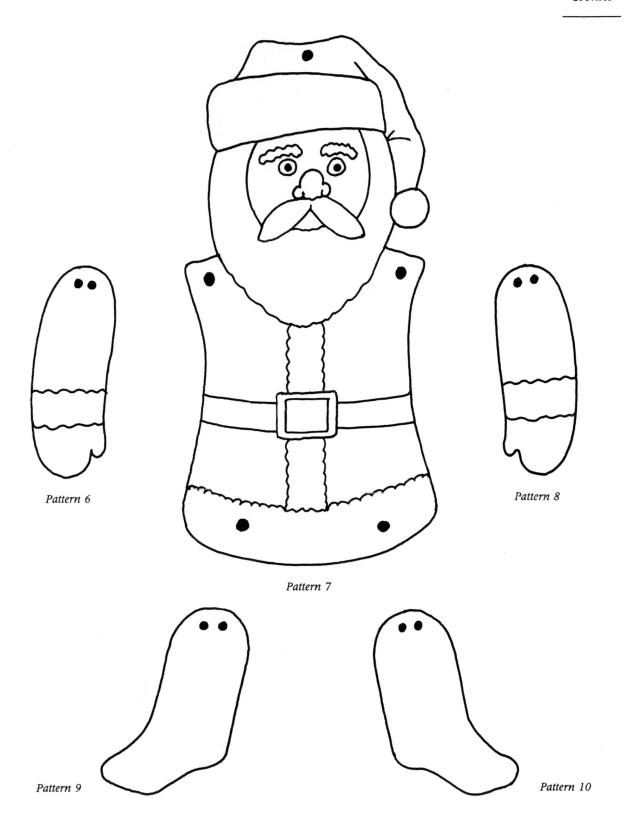

Pattern 6

Pattern 8

Pattern 7

Pattern 9

Pattern 10

Raggedy Ann

Bake the pattern pieces shown (patterns 11–15). Thin 3 tablespoons of royal icing with a few drops of water. Using a small paintbrush, brush the icing on the arms, legs, and dress, as indicated in the photograph. Tint the remaining thinned icing pink and brush on the hands and face. Tint the thinned pink icing black and brush on the feet.

Tint about 3 tablespoons of royal icing orange, using red and yellow coloring. Using the #2 tip, pipe curly hair around the face. Tint the remaining orange icing red and pipe horizontal stripes on the legs above the black area, with the #2 tip. Set aside any remaining red icing for the nose and mouth, keeping it tightly covered so it will not dry out.

Tint about a tablespoon of icing blue and pipe small dots with the #2 tip on the arms, along the hem of the skirt, and below the chin on the dress, as indicated in the photograph. Pipe fold lines below the blue dots on the front of the dress.

Pipe 2 white dots for the eyes. Tint about a tablespoon of the icing black and, using the #1 tip, pipe eyebrows, dots in the center of the eyes, eyelashes, the mouth, and a wavy line along the hem.

With the #46 tip, pipe a white horizontal line for the waist and 2 vertical lines above it for the straps of the dress.

Next, holding the wide end of the #101 tip toward the cookie and the narrow end facing out and up, pipe a white ruffle under the chin and on the end of the sleeve on each arm.

To finish the face, using the reserved red icing and the #1 tip, pipe a small triangle in the center for the nose and a short line in the center of the mouth for the lips.

Let the icing dry completely before tying the pieces together with pink ribbon.

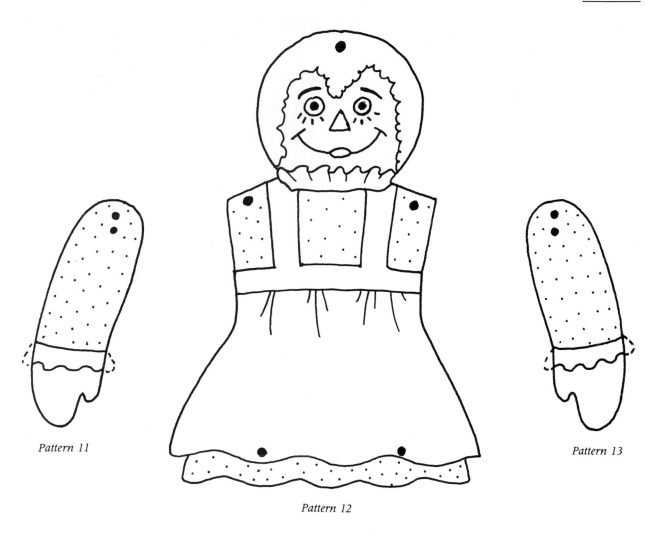

Pattern 11

Pattern 12

Pattern 13

Pattern 14

Pattern 15

Raggedy Andy

Bake the pattern pieces shown (patterns 16–20). Thin about 3 tablespoons of royal icing with a few drops of water. Using a small paintbrush, brush the white icing on the arms, legs, and body as indicated in the photograph. Tint the remaining thinned icing pink and brush on the hands and face. Tint the pink icing black and brush it on the feet.

Tint another tablespoon of icing blue and thin it with water. Brush on the tops of the legs and the area of the body for the overalls, including the straps.

Pipe a white collar just below the chin with the #46 tip. Then pipe 2 buttons with the #2 tip and white icing at the bottom of the overall straps. Pipe 2 white dots for the eyes.

Tint 2 tablespoons of icing orange, using red and yellow coloring. Pipe hair around the face, as with Raggedy Ann. Tint the remaining orange icing red and, using the #2 tip, pipe dots on the shirt and horizontal stripes on the socks. Save any remaining red icing for the mouth and nose.

Tint 2 tablespoons of royal icing black. Pipe a black bow just below the chin with the #2 tip, then decorate the face in the same manner as with Raggedy Ann. Let the icing dry completely before tying the pieces together with blue ribbon.

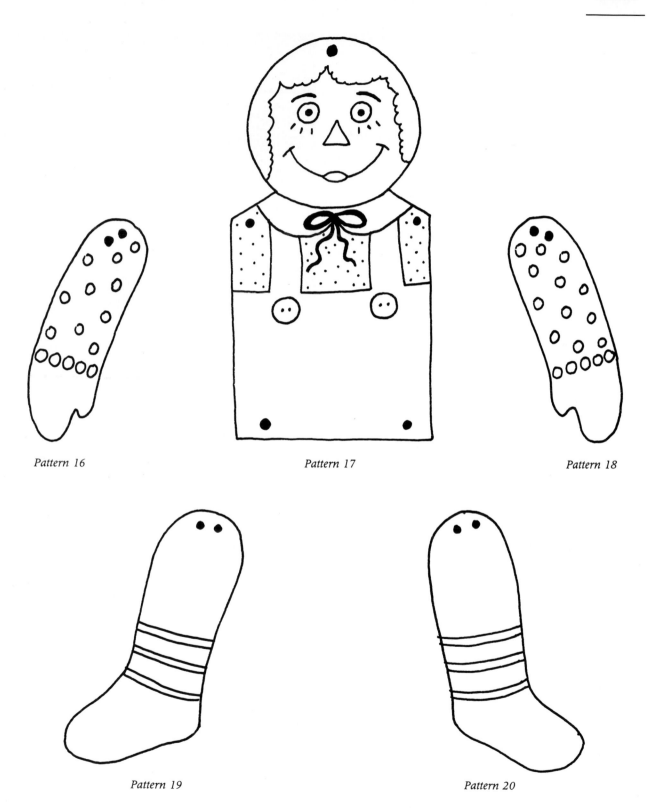

Pattern 16

Pattern 17

Pattern 18

Pattern 19

Pattern 20

The Nutcracker

Bake the pattern pieces shown (patterns 21–24). Make 2 of the arm pieces. Thin 3 tablespoons of royal icing with a few drops of water and tint it pink. Using a small paintbrush, paint the face and hands. Tint the remaining pink icing red and brush on the areas indicated in the photograph. Tint the remaining red icing black and brush on the boot area and across the middle for the belt.

Tint 1 teaspoon of icing blue and thin it with a few drops of water. Brush blue icing on the top of the hat and the small triangle just below the belt. Let the cookies dry completely.

Tint 3 tablespoons of icing yellow and pipe lines on the shoulders with the #2 tip. While the icing is still wet, sprinkle it with yellow sugar. Pipe yellow zigzags just above the hands, for the cuffs, and sprinkle them with sugar. Pipe dots for the buttons and a square for the belt buckle and sprinkle them with yellow sugar.

Thin the remaining yellow icing with a few drops of water and fill in the areas on the legs and hat. Sprinkle yellow nonpareils over the wet icing on the legs and yellow sugar over the icing on the hat.

Pipe white lines with the #2 tip for the hair and beard. Pipe 2 dots for the eyes and 3 dots for the teeth.

Tint 1 tablespoon of royal icing black. To finish, pipe black eyebrows, a dot in the center of each eye, and a mustache. Tint 1 tablespoon of royal icing pink. Pipe a pink nose with the #2 tip.

Let the icing dry completely before tying the pieces together with red, yellow, and blue ribbon.

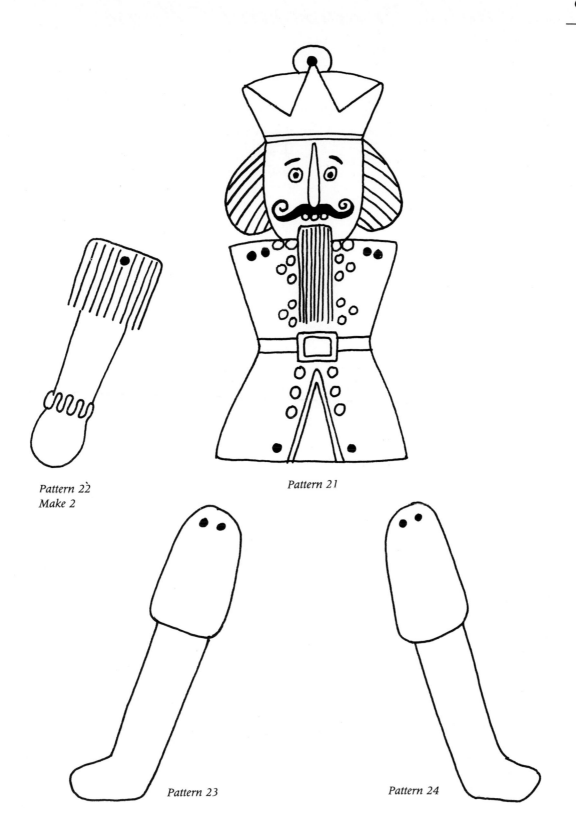

Pattern 22
Make 2

Pattern 21

Pattern 23

Pattern 24

Swiss Chalet Gingerbread House

THE SMELL of gingerbread always makes me think of Christmas. The gingerbread house is a classic holiday confection, and this cozy little Alpine house is an easy-to-construct project that the whole family will enjoy making.

cardboard
2 recipes gingerbread-house dough (page 150)
rolling pin
sharp knife
parchment paper
3 recipes royal icing (page 145)

nontoxic marking pen
green, red, blue, brown, purple, and black paste food coloring
X-acto knife
10 large silver dragées
small silver dragées
9 × 12–inch foamcore board
palette knife or spatula
pastry bags and couplers
tips #1, #2, #17, and #104
clear edible glitter

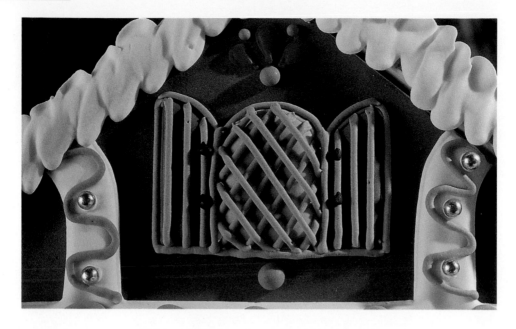

Enlarge the patterns given (patterns 1–4) to twice their size. Transfer the pieces onto cardboard and cut out. Prepare the gingerbread dough according to directions. Roll the dough out on aluminum foil on a cookie sheet to about ¼ inch thick. Place the pattern pieces on the dough and carefully cut them out with a sharp knife. Make two each of the side and roof pieces. Reroll scraps of dough. Bake as directed in the gingerbread recipe. When you remove the baked cookies from the oven, place the pattern pieces on top and trim off any excess dough with a sharp knife. Let the cookies cool completely on wire racks.

To decorate the house:

The house pieces are decorated before the house is assembled. Using the enlarged pattern pieces, transfer the designs onto the baked dough with the sharp end of an X-acto knife or a non-toxic marking pen in a light color. Outline the designs with icing, using the #1 tip. Pipe all of the outlines in one color at the same time. The white designs are outlined in white, the red designs in red, and so on. The small pink and red dots do not need to be outlined.

Make 2 recipes of royal icing, place it in 5 bowls in the following amounts, and tint accordingly: ¾ cup green, ¾ cup red, ½ cup pink, ½ cup blue, and ½ cup pale purple. Keep the bowls of tinted icing and the extra icing covered with a lid or a damp cloth while you are working.

After all of the designs have been outlined, thin each color and ½ cup of the white icing with a few drops of water until a spoonful of icing dropped into the bowl disappears in 10 seconds. Using the #2 tip, fill each colored outline with thinned icing. Place the small dragées in the wet icing in the roof designs, and on the front and back white areas as indicated in the photograph. Let all of the decorations dry for a few hours.

When the decorations are dry, tint 1 cup of the white unthinned icing light brown and pipe the light-brown trim as shown, using the #2 tip. Mix black coloring into any leftover color and pipe black hinges on the doors and windows.

To assemble the house:

In the center of the foamcore board, outline a 5 × 8–inch rectangle with a pencil. The 8-inch line should be parallel to the 12-inch side, and the 5-inch line should be parallel to the 9-inch side. Make another recipe of royal icing. Fill a pastry bag with white icing and fit it with a #17 tip. Pipe a line of icing along the bottom of the front gingerbread panel and stand the iced edge on one of the 5-inch pencil lines, pressing gently. To keep the panel upright, prop a can or glass on either side to hold it in place. Pipe a line of icing inside the right-side edge of the front panel. Pipe a line of icing on the bottom edge of one of the side panels. Press the side panel onto the board, lining up the bottom along the 8-inch pencil line and the left-side edge against the iced edge of the front panel. Add the other 2 pieces in the same way. Use cans or glasses to support the house sides while they are drying.

After the four walls are completed, let the house dry for a few hours or overnight before adding the roof. If the seams are still wet when you add the roof, its weight may cause the house to collapse. Keep the cans or glasses in place while the house is drying, and also on the outside while you add the roof. (Make sure there are no glasses inside the house when you add the roof, or they will be permanently enclosed.)

To construct the roof, pipe a line of icing along the top edges of the two sides and the front and back pieces. Also pipe a line of icing on the top edge of one of the roof pieces. Place each roof panel in the icing, making sure that the tops meet at the center points of the house. Press the roof panels together and hold them until the icing sets and the roof pieces do not move. Let the roof set for a few hours.

To finish the house, pipe a zigzag line of white icing along the peak of the roof and place 10 large dragées, evenly spaced, in the wet icing. Pipe a vertical zigzag line of icing up each corner of the house. Using the #104 tip, pipe a ruffle edge around the top of the front and back. Pipe a ruffle edge along the eaves of the roof. Thin about 1 cup of white royal icing and, using a knife or spatula, spread it over the visible parts of the foamcore board. Sprinkle with clear edible glitter.

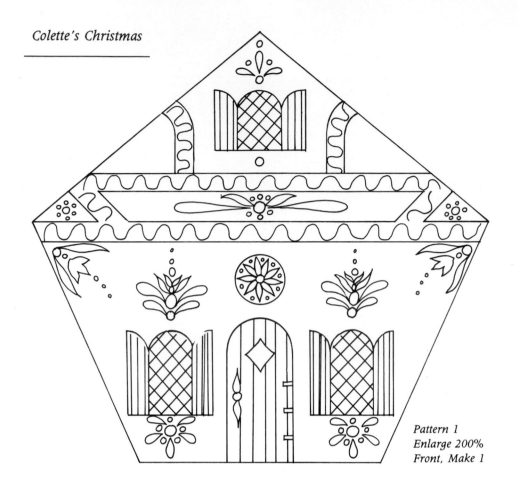

Pattern 1
Enlarge 200%
Front, Make 1

Pattern 2
Enlarge 200%
Sides, Make 2

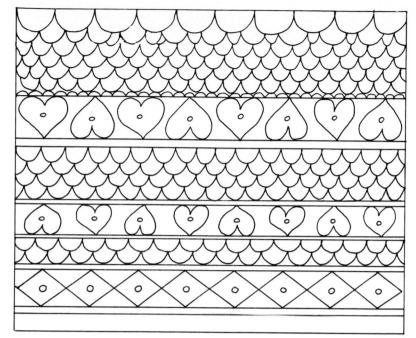

Pattern 3
Enlarge 200%
Roof, Make 2

Pattern 4
Enlarge 200%
Back, Make 1

Cookie Gift Boxes

I ORIGINALLY came up with this idea for *Ladies' Home Journal.* Cookie boxes are a simple alternative to gingerbread houses. You can fill the boxes with sweet treats and give them as gifts or use them as a holiday centerpiece.

Makes 2 large or 3 small boxes

To make the cookie boxes:
1 recipe basic cookie dough (page 149)
heavy cardboard or foamcore board
X-acto knife
metal ruler
sharp kitchen knife
flour for dusting surface
greased cookie sheets
wax paper
1 recipe royal icing (page 145)
pastry bag and coupler
tip #15

Pattern sizes for boxes:
Small cube: 1 top: 2¼ × 2¼ inches
    4 sides: 2¼ × 2½ inches
    1 bottom: 1⅞ × 1⅞ inches
Medium cube: 5 sides and top: 4 × 4 inches
    1 bottom: 3¾ × 3¾ inches
Large cube: 1 top: 4½ × 4½ inches
    4 sides: 4½ × 5 inches
    1 bottom: 4 × 4 inches
Large rectangle: 1 top: 3½ × 5½ inches
    2 sides: 3½ × 2 inches
    2 sides: 2 × 5½ inches
    1 bottom: 3¼ × 5¼ inches
Tall rectangle: 1 top: 2¾ × 2¾ inches
    4 sides: 2¾ × 5¾ inches
    1 bottom: 2⅜ × 2⅜ inches

Preheat the oven to 350 degrees F. Draw the patterns for the boxes, using the dimensions above, on a piece of thick cardboard or foamcore. Cut out the patterns carefully, using an X-acto knife and a ruler.

Roll out the chilled dough onto a floured surface to ¼ inch thick. Place the pattern pieces on top of the dough and, using a sharp knife, cut out each piece in the number required to make a complete box. Carefully place the cutout pieces on a greased cookie sheet. Bake for 10–12 minutes or until golden brown.

Remove one piece at a time from the cookie sheet, placing the cardboard pattern on top of the baked piece and trimming if necessary. This must be done while the cookie is still warm, or it may crack. Place the cookies on a wire rack and cool completely.

Using a kitchen knife, bevel the 2 side edges of each of the side pieces (fig. 1), holding the knife at a 45-degree angle, with the point toward the back of the cookie, and carefully shaving the edge a little at a time to avoid cracking. Do not bevel the top or the bottom piece.

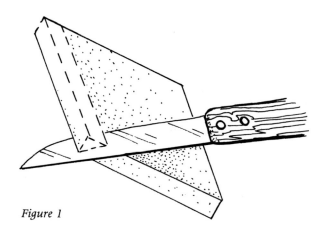

Figure 1

To construct the box, place the bottom cookie piece on a sheet of wax paper. Fill a pastry bag with royal icing and fit it with the #15 tip. Pipe a thick line of icing along one edge of the cookie. Place an unbeveled edge of a side piece against the icing so that the side and bottom are at right angles to each other, with the beveled edges facing inward. Press the two pieces together tightly. Place a glass or cup up against the upright piece to support it while you are working. Pipe another line of icing along the edge of the bottom piece adjacent to the first one. Pipe another line of icing up the side of the upright piece, inside the beveled edge. Press the beveled edge of the second side piece into the icing. Continue until the box is complete. Support the sides with glasses until the icing sets, about 2 hours. In some of the box designs the lids are attached, and in some they aren't, so add the lids according to the specific directions.

To make the designs shown:

All of the designs are decorated with royal icing. When the directions call for thinned royal icing, add a few drops of water to the icing until it reaches the consistency of corn syrup. The icing can then be spread over the surface with a metal spatula or knife, or piped through a piping bag with a small tip, such as a #2 or #3, attached. The edges can be finished with a small, soft paintbrush or a knife.

Marbleized Box

large rectangle cookie box
1 recipe royal icing (page 145)
wax paper
pastry bag and coupler
tips #4 and #48
red food coloring
toothpicks

Make the white icing bow on wax paper, as directed in the section on royal-icing bows (page 156), using the #48 tip. Construct the box and let it dry completely. Do not attach the lid. Add red coloring to ¾ cup royal icing and thin. Fill a pastry bag with white icing and fit it with the #4 tip. Turn the box on its side and cover the side facing up with thinned red icing, using a knife to spread it. Immediately pipe white icing in squiggles onto the wet red icing. With a toothpick, drag the white icing through the red icing to marbleize. Let the icing dry and repeat on all sides and the top. Finish the edges of the lid with red icing, so that none of the cookie shows. When the box and lid are completely dry, attach the lid to the box with a little royal icing. Using the #48 tip, pipe a white ribbon across the front and one side of the box. Attach the bow onto the end of the lid that the ribbon crosses with a dab of royal icing.

the ot
and a
tube
tip on
one o
red ge
icing.
a toot
that ea
Then
gel (fi
each f
    Re
pieces
pletely
    Co
tions,
the bo
der alo
using
tach th
hold it

Figure 3

Co

X|

mec
1 re
gree
3 p;
tips

Con
Do 1
dry,
squa
knife
part
part
dam
icing
T
the :
left o
in th
right
thinr
pipee
with
plete
the s

Red and White Plaid Box

tall rectangle cookie box
1 recipe royal icing (page 145)
wax paper
red paste coloring
pastry bag and coupler
tips #5, #48, and #61

Using the #61 tip, make a red icing bow on wax paper, as directed in the section on royal-icing bows (page 156), and let it dry. Construct the cookie box and let it dry completely. Do not attach the lid. Thin ½ cup of royal icing. Turn the box on its side and cover the side facing up with the icing. Allow each side to dry before turning the box to ice the next side. Place the box on its side again. Tint the remaining icing red.

Pipe 5 horizontal lines with the red icing and the #48 tip across the side facing up, following the

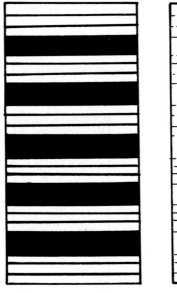

Figure 5   *Figure 6*

diagram for the spacing of the lines. Pipe smaller red lines with the #5 tip in between the thicker lines, again using the diagram for placement (fig. 5). Finally, pipe 5 vertical lines across the horizontal lines, spacing them evenly (fig. 6). Let dry completely. Repeat on all 4 sides and the lid. Place the bow on top of the lid, using a dab of royal icing to attach it.

Small Striped Box

small cube cookie box
½ recipe royal icing (page 145)
red, green, and yellow paste food coloring
wax paper
3 pastry bags and couplers
tips #3, #47, and #59

Using the #59 tip, make a small red bow on wax paper, as directed in the section on royal-icing bows (page 156), and let it dry completely. Construct the cookie box and let it dry completely. Do not attach the lid. Add red coloring to ¼ cup icing and thin. Turn the box on its side and cover the side facing up with the thinned red icing. Let the first side dry before turning the box. Cover all of the sides and the lid with red icing.

Tint ½ cup of the royal icing green and ¼ cup yellow. Turn the box on its side and pipe 4 green vertical stripes, evenly spaced, using the #47 tip, with the flat side of the tip facing up. Then pipe a yellow stripe on either side of each green stripe, using the #3 tip. Repeat for each side of the box, letting the icing dry before continuing on to the next side. The lid is decorated the same as the sides. Attach the bow to the lid with a dab of royal icing.

Christmas Tree Box

large cube cookie box
sharp knife
ruler
1 recipe royal icing (page 145)
red and green paste food coloring
pastry bags and couplers
tips #2 and #3
clear piping gel
small paintbrush
gold dragées

Construct the box and let it dry completely. Do not attach the lid to the box. On each side and the lid of the box, find the center of the top edge. Using the point of a knife and a ruler, draw a line connecting each lower corner to the middle point (fig. 7). This will make a Christmas-tree formation. With the ruler and knife, mark off ½-inch intervals from the top of each side to the bottom, then draw horizontal lines across each side at these ½-inch marks (figs. 8 and 9).

Divide the royal icing into 3 parts. Tint one part green, another part red, and leave the third part white. Thin the green icing. Fill a pastry bag with 3 heaping tablespoons of red icing and fit on the #2 tip. Thin the rest of the red icing. Placing the box on its side, outline the tree shape and the horizontal lines marked on the *outside* of the tree with red icing. With the thinned red icing, fill in the tree shape. Fill in every other stripe on the outside

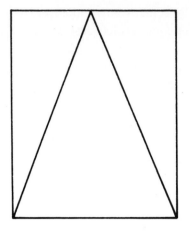

Figure 7

Figure 8

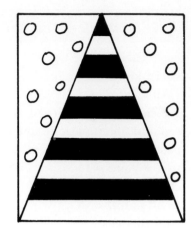

Figure 9

of the tree with green. The alternate stripes are filled with gold dragées. Brush piping gel into the stripe areas that are not green, and sprinkle the dragées in the gel. Let the box dry for an hour, then turn the box onto its next side. On this side, the stripes are on the *inside* of the tree, and the area outside of the tree is solid red. Fill in every other stripe with green, as you did on the first side. Brush piping gel on the alternate stripes and

sprinkle dragées over the gel. Repeat these 2 alternating patterns on the other 2 sides, then choose one of the patterns for the lid.

When all of the sides and the lid have dried, go back and pipe white dots in the solid red areas of the trees or the background, using the #2 tip. Finish the sides of the lids with either red or green icing, so that none of the cookie shows.

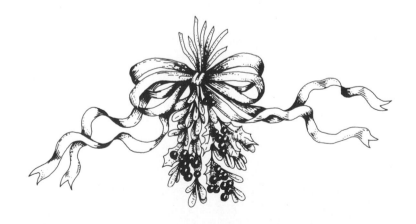

Pumpkin-Seed and Nonpareil Box

large rectangle cookie box
1 recipe royal icing (page 145)
white nonpareils
tweezers
green pumpkin seeds
gold dragées
pastry bag and coupler
tip #2

Construct the cookie box and let it dry completely. Do not attach the lid. Thin ¾ cup royal icing. Turn the box on its side and cover the side with thinned white icing. Immediately sprinkle the entire surface with the nonpareils. (*Hint:* It's a good idea to place the box in a cake pan or some type of shallow container so that the nonpareils don't bounce onto the floor. The nonpareils that fall into the cake pan can be reused, thus avoiding a lot of

waste and crunching under your feet.) Let dry completely before turning the box. Cover all the sides, the lid, and the sides of the lid. Let dry.

With tweezers, decorate the lid and sides with pumpkin seeds and gold dragées as shown, using the #2 tip and dots of stiff white royal icing to secure them (figs. 10, 11, and 12).

Figure 10
Side

Figure 11
Top

Figure 12
Side

Blue Dragée Box

½ recipe royal icing (page 145)
wax paper
small cube cookie box
pastry bag and coupler
tips #3 and #48
sky-blue food coloring
large and small silver dragées

Using the #48 tip, make a white bow on wax paper, as directed in the section on royal-icing bows (page 156), and let it dry completely. Construct the cookie box and attach the lid to the box with a small amount of royal icing. Let the box dry completely. You will need about ¾ cup thinned light-blue royal icing. Cover the lid with the thinned icing, spreading it on with a knife. Immediately sprinkle large and small dragées onto the wet icing and let the icing dry for about an hour. Turn the box on its side. Spread thinned icing on the side facing up and sprinkle with dragées, in the same manner as the lid. Let the icing dry completely, then turn the box again so that the next side is facing up. Repeat with icing and dragées, letting each side dry before turning. When the entire box is dry, attach the bow to the top of the box with a dab of royal icing.

Home Sweet Home

THIS IS A REPLICA of the Brooklyn house I live in. It was originally a one-family home, built in the late 1800s, and has since been divided into two apartment buildings. Mine has been owned by the Riccardelli family since the 1950s. I have always loved this house and thought it would be a great tribute to its stately design to make a miniature of it in cookie dough.

3 recipes basic cookie dough (page 149)
cardboard
rolling pin
parchment paper
sharp knife
18-inch ruler
X-acto knife
cardboard tube from paper towel roll
compass
foamcore
vegetable shortening
metal bowl, 5¾ inches in diameter (can be
    found at kitchen equipment stores)
16½-inch-square foamcore board, two layers
    thick
⅜-inch-wide white ribbon
glue
3 recipes royal icing (page 145)
brown, red, green, and black paste food coloring
pastry bags and couplers
tips #2, #3, and #17
16 ounces whole almonds
7 ice cream cones
wax paper
mini–Fun Chips or small colored candies
clear edible glitter

Make the cookie dough and refrigerate for a few hours. Preheat the oven to 350 degrees F. Enlarge pattern pieces 1–34 to 150 percent of their size and transfer patterns 1–26 and 30–34 onto cardboard. Roll the dough directly onto cookie sheets lined with parchment paper. Place the pattern pieces on top and cut out the shapes with a sharp knife as specified. Reserve the scraps of leftover dough.

To make the embossed patterns on the front and porch panels, press the ruler into the dough horizontally, first ½ inch from the bottom and then ⅛ inch above that. Continue embossing lines on the panels at alternating ½-inch and ⅛-inch intervals (see patterns 4, 14, and 22). Then place the pattern on top of the dough again and trim off any excess.

Make the embossed brick pattern for the other 3 panels and the chimneys. Emboss the horizontal lines first with the ruler, at 1-inch intervals. Then add vertical lines, using a knife, to make a brick pattern (see patterns 1, 2, 3, and 5).

Cut out all the windows with an X-acto knife.

Bake all the pieces for about 10 minutes, or until golden brown. Watch the smaller pieces carefully because they bake much faster than the large pieces.

To make the turret, cut a paper towel tube in half lengthwise, then cut the halves crosswise so that each one is 8½ inches long. Use the compass to draw two circles 2⅞ inches in diameter on a piece of foamcore, then cut out the circles and cut them in half. Place two of the semicircles inside each half-tube for support. (The tubes will sit in the oven with the flat side down.) Cut a piece of parchment paper to fit over each tube precisely. Roll out the dough, then place the parchment on top. Cut out two pieces of dough the same size as the paper. Turn over one piece of dough along with its paper backing. Emboss the same pattern as on the front panel (pattern 4) and cut out the windows on *1* piece only. Place the dough and its paper backing on the cardboard tube and bake. Let the baked pieces cool completely on the tube before you remove them. *Important:* After baking any piece of the house, always place the pattern on top of the baked pieces again to make sure that the dough has not spread. If necessary, trim the warm cookies with an X-acto knife.

For the domed roof, cut out eight wedges according to the pattern (pattern 10). Rub a thin coat of shortening on the outside of a 5¾-inch-wide bowl. Turn the bowl upside down and place the dough wedges point side up around the bowl. Bake on the upside-down bowl until golden brown. Let them cool completely on the bowl. Remove the cooled pieces from the bowl.

To make the porch columns, roll the remaining dough into a long cylinder about ⅜ inch wide. Cut it into 12 2-inch cylinders. Place 2 columns side by side on the parchment-lined cookie sheet and repeat to form 6 columns (use pattern 26 as a guide). Bake.

To assemble the house:

Make 1 recipe of royal icing at a time, as needed. Cover the bowl with a damp cloth to keep the icing from drying out. Tint the icing light brown to match the color of the cookies as closely as possible.

To make the turret, glue the two cylinder halves together by piping a line of icing with the #17 tip along the 2 long edges of one piece and then pressing the other piece against it. Dry the turret upright for a few hours before adding it to the house.

Glue ribbon around the edge of the 16½-inch-square piece of foamcore. Use a pencil to draw a 9 × 10¾–inch rectangle on the foamcore, with the 10¾-inch side parallel to and 1 inch from the back of the board. Center the rectangle left and right (see fig. 1). Starting with the back edge of the inside rectangle, pipe a line of icing with the #17 tip along the pencil line for the back of the house. Stand the back panel (pattern 1) centered on the line in the icing. Prop some bottles or cans on both sides to hold it in place. Pipe a line of icing along the right adjacent line on the board and up the right edge of the back panel. Place the corresponding side panel (pattern 2) in the icing and press it in place, propping it up with more bottles. Attach the left side panel (pattern 3) in the same way as the right side panel.

Attach the front panel (pattern 4) to the front edge of the right side panel, along the front pencil line.

To place the chimneys, pipe a line of icing up the side panels in the areas marked on the pattern, then attach the chimneys (pattern 5).

To attach the turret, line up the right seam of the turret with the left edge of the house front, and the back of the turret with the front edge of the left side piece. Pipe icing along these edges and on the bottom and press the turret to the board.

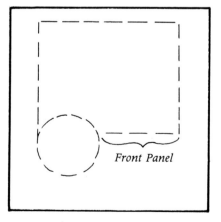

Figure 1

Next, add the roof. Start by attaching the back roof panel (pattern 6) with icing on the back side of the house. Add the top roof panel (also pattern 6) and then the front piece (pattern 7). The front of the roof has a slight overhang. Next, attach the gabled roofs (patterns 8 and 9).

Assemble the domed turret roof. Use icing to attach a curved wedge (pattern 10), wide end down, onto the back rim of the turret. At the same time, attach a second wedge onto the opposite front rim so that the wedges meet at the top and support each other. Pipe a dot of icing under the tips for added support (fig. 2). Let them dry for an hour. Attach the remaining wedges evenly spaced around the rim, with all of their tips meeting at the center point. Pipe icing to fill in the gaps between the wedges. Let them dry completely.

Tint 4 tablespoons of icing red, then thin about 2 tablespoons of the red. Cover the doors (pattern 11) with thinned red icing and let them dry for an hour. Decorate the doors with unthinned

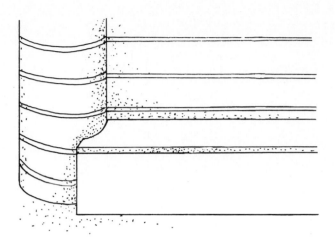

Figure 3

red piped lines from the #2 tip, as indicated on the pattern.

To construct the porch, pipe brown icing on the 2 long edges and the curve of the floor piece (pattern 12) and on the two long edges of the porch front (pattern 13). Place them at right angles to each other with the floor piece on top of the front piece and against the house (fig. 3). Attach one of the embossed porch sections (pattern 14) to the right end of the porch. Attach another embossed section to the porch right front. Attach the right railing (pattern 15) perpendicular to the porch. Stack the stairs (patterns 16–21) next to the railing and against the porch, gluing them together with icing. Then add the left railing (pattern 15). Add the remaining embossed porch sections (pattern 14) and stairs along the rest of the porch front. Attach the last embossed section to the left end of the porch (pattern 22).

Attach the doors (pattern 11) to the front of the house, in line with the stairs and sitting on the floor of the porch.

Attach the rails (patterns 23, 24, and 25) to the top edge of the porch. Then glue the columns in place and let them dry for about 2 hours before adding the porch roof.

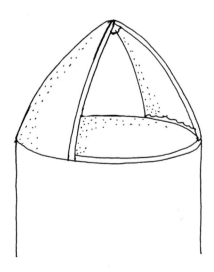

Figure 2

While the icing is drying, cut the almonds carefully in half lengthwise, along the seam, with an X-acto knife.

Pipe the wrought-iron fence sections (patterns 27, 28, and 29) on wax paper with black icing and the #2 tip. Let dry.

Pipe 16 candles for the windows on wax paper, using the patterns on the front house section (pattern 4) as a guide. Use the #2 tip with red icing for the candles, and the same tip with green icing for the bases.

Start to cover the roof with almonds. Pipe a dot of icing on the roof and attach an almond, with the flat side down and the narrow end pointing up. Start at the front of the roof and make one row at a time. Overlap the next row about halfway over the first. Cover the front roof, the turret, and the top and back roof pieces.

Add the porch roof (pattern 30) by piping a dot of icing on the tops of each of the columns and a line of icing on the back and curved edge of the roof piece. Press the roof gently onto the columns and against the front of the house just below the lower windows. Cover with almonds.

Pipe light-brown icing in a zigzag motion along all of the seams, using the #3 tip. Pipe black borders around all of the windows, except for the windows in the front section. These are outlined with light-brown icing. Use the #3 tip for all of these outlines.

To make the windowpane divisions, use black icing and the #2 tip. Attach the icing at the end of the tip to the top center of each window. Let the icing flow out of the bag, and at the same time, move the tip down to the bottom of the window. Attach the icing to the bottom of the window. Let it dry for an hour. Pipe a horizontal line of icing across each window, using the patterns as a guide. Pipe brown divisions in the windows outlined in brown icing.

Pipe brown zigzags around the front windows, along the porch rails, and along the tops of the turret windows.

To make the trees, place each ice cream cone on wax paper. Using green icing and the #17 tip, place the tip at the bottom of the cone and squeeze, applying pressure as you pull out so that the icing comes to a point. Continue making branches in this way around and up the cone, until it is covered. Add colored candies to the wet icing while you are working. To make trees of different heights, carefully break off the open ends of some of the cones.

Spread thinned gray icing on the board with a metal spatula. Place the pieces for the low wall (patterns 31–34) upright around the house, lining them up with the bottoms of the stairs in the wet icing. Arrange the trees around the house inside the low wall, using dots of icing to hold them in place. Carefully place the wrought-iron fence on top of the wall, using dots of brown icing to hold it in place.

Tint ½ cup of icing light-green and pipe zigzag lines with the #2 tip along the edges of the roof and on the front of the house (see photograph). Arrange colored mini–Fun Chips in the wet icing, evenly spaced.

Attach the candles to the front of the windows, using the photograph as a guide.

Finally, pipe snow and icicles on the roof and sidewalk with the #3 tip and white icing. Sprinkle edible glitter on the wet icing. Then take a long winter's nap.

Pattern 3
Enlarge 150%
Left Side, Make 1

Back of House

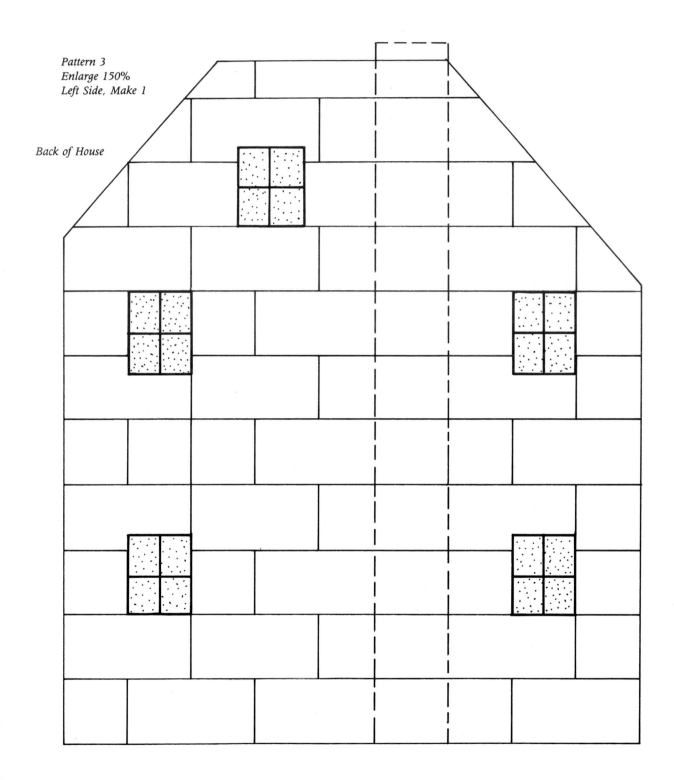

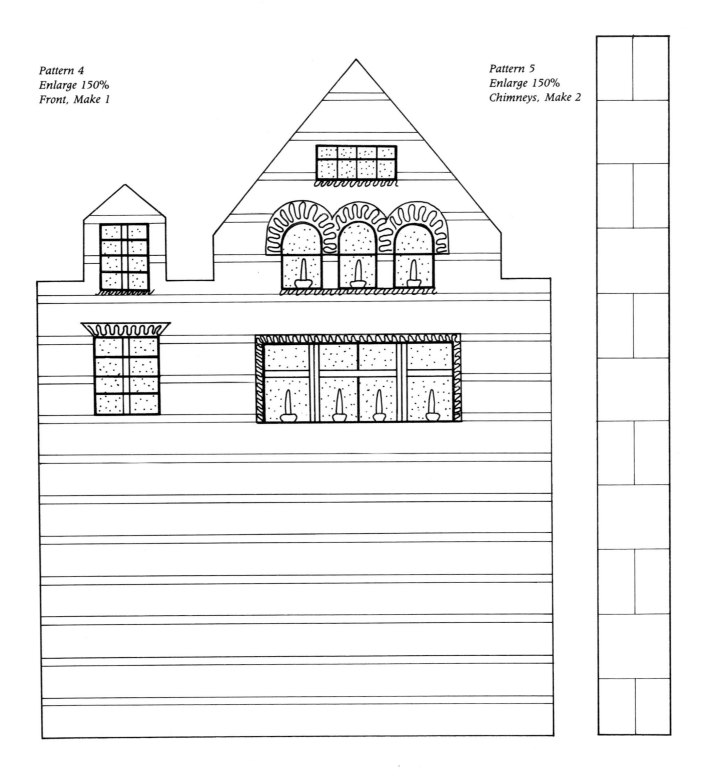

Pattern 4
Enlarge 150%
Front, Make 1

Pattern 5
Enlarge 150%
Chimneys, Make 2

Patter
Enlar
Side o

Patter
Enlar
Fence,

Pies

Choc...

*P*UMPKIN P...
Since I like to d...
combining choc...
create a visual t...
to do, and the r...

Makes one 9-inch

chocolate pie cr...
9-inch pie plate
rolling pin
wax paper
pumpkin pie fill...
1 pound *total* wh...
    chocolate (⅓...
cookie sheets
metal spatula
aluminum foil
variety of flower,...

Chocolate ...

1 cup all-purpose
⅛ teaspoon salt
3 tablespoons uns...
⅓ cup sugar
4 tablespoons cold
4 tablespoons cold
2 tablespoons ice w...
rolling pin

Combine the flour, s...
bowl. Cut in the but...
pastry blender or 2 k...
are formed. Add the...
time, and mix until t...
Shape the dough int...
Wrap in plastic and r...

While people love to bake pies at Christmastime, they usually don't think of decorating them. Here are some festive ideas for decorated pies to grace your holiday dessert table.

Apple-Cranberry Holiday Pie

*C*RANBERRIES and apples are traditional holiday flavors and combine to make a fresh-tasting, tart pie filling. I decorate the top crust with pieces of dough that I have cut into a design and painted with food coloring.

Makes one 10-inch pie

1 recipe basic pie crust (recipe below)
apple-cranberry filling (recipe below)
rolling pin
10-inch tart pan
wax paper
sharp knife
1 egg yolk
red, green, and purple liquid food coloring
small paintbrush

Basic Pie Crust

2½ cups all-purpose flour
¼ teaspoon salt
2 teaspoons sugar
10 tablespoons cold butter
6 tablespoons vegetable shortening
6 tablespoons ice water

All of the ingredients should be cold. Place the flour, salt, and sugar in a bowl. Cut in the butter and shortening with a pastry blender or 2 knives until pea-sized pieces are formed. Add the ice water, a teaspoon at a time, and mix just until the dough holds together. The dough should not be sticky. Divide the dough into 2 equal portions. Shape each into a ball and flatten slightly. Wrap in plastic or wax paper and refrigerate for at least an hour.

Apple-Cranberry Filling

2 pounds apples (2 Granny Smith or other tart apples and 3 Yellow Delicious)
¾ cup dried cranberries *or* halved fresh or frozen cranberries plus 2 tablespoons sugar
1 tablespoon flour
⅓ cup sugar
2 tablespoons brown sugar
¼ teaspoon cinnamon
⅛ teaspoon nutmeg
1 to 2 tablespoons butter

Preheat the oven to 400 degrees F. Peel and core the apples and slice them into pieces ⅛ to ¼ inch thick. Combine all of the ingredients except the butter and toss gently.

Roll out one ball of dough between 2 pieces of wax paper into a 12-inch circle. Fit the dough into a 10-inch tart pan. Trim the excess around the edge of the pan, reserving the scraps. Spoon the filling evenly onto the bottom crust. Roll out the remaining ball of dough into an 11-inch circle for the top crust. Place the dough over the filling and trim off the excess. Press the 2 edges together. Roll out the scraps on a lightly floured surface to about ⅛ inch thick. Enlarge pattern 1 to 125 percent of

its size. Cut ou
arrange them
little water to

Mix an egg
the mixture in

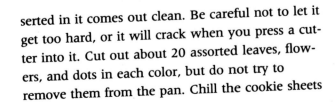

serted in it comes out clean. Be careful not to let it get too hard, or it will crack when you press a cutter into it. Cut out about 20 assorted leaves, flowers, and dots in each color, but do not try to remove them from the pan. Chill the cookie sheets until the chocolate is cold, then peel them off the foil with a metal spatula.

Remelt the remaining chocolate scraps and drizzle over the cutouts with a fork. Arrange the cutouts on the pie to form a wreath.

Christmas No-Bake Cheesecake

RASPBERRY AND LIME are combined to make this delicious and elegant cheesecake. No baking is necessary — simply chill, and you will have a dessert with a smooth, chiffonlike texture that will melt in your mouth.

1 vanilla wafer crumb crust (recipe below)
9-inch springform pan
4 large eggs, separated and at room temperature
1 cup sugar, divided into ¾ cup and ¼ cup
1 cup heavy cream
24 ounces cream cheese, at room temperature
1 teaspoon lemon extract
½ teaspoon vanilla extract
¼ cup lime juice
1 tablespoon unflavored gelatin
⅛ teaspoon cream of tartar
1 cup sour cream
green and pink food coloring
2 heaping tablespoons seedless raspberry jam
pastry bag and coupler
tip #6
raspberry candies for decoration

Vanilla Wafer Crumb Crust

1½ cups vanilla wafers, crushed
¼ cup melted butter

Preheat the oven to 350 degrees F. To make the wafer crumbs, place the cookies in a plastic bag and roll over them with a rolling pin *or* crush them in a blender for a few seconds. Combine the crumbs and butter and press into the bottom of the 9-inch pan. Bake for 12 minutes and let cool on a rack. Grease the sides of the pan with butter and set aside. Just before you are ready to add the filling, place the pan in the freezer so that the mixture will adhere when you pipe the design on the sides of the pan.

Beat the egg yolks with an electric mixer until they are pale yellow. Beat in ¾ cup sugar on medium speed until the mixture forms a ribbon when the beaters are lifted. In a saucepan, bring the cream just to the boiling point. Remove from the heat and slowly add it to the egg mixture, beating continuously on low. Return the mixture to the saucepan and cook over low heat, stirring constantly until the mixture thickens and is just about to boil. Remove from the heat and transfer to a bowl to cool.

Cream the cheese with the mixer, then add the cooled egg mixture. Beat on low until well combined. Add the lemon and vanilla extracts.

Place the lime juice in a small saucepan and sprinkle the gelatin over it. Let the gelatin soften for 5 minutes. Place the pan on low heat and stir until the gelatin dissolves. Immediately remove from the heat. *Do not boil.* Add the gelatin to the cheese mixture and stir until it is totally incorporated. Set aside.

Beat the egg whites with the electric mixer on high until they are foamy, then add the cream of tartar and beat on high until soft peaks form. Slowly add the remaining ¼ cup sugar while beating on medium speed. Beat on high until stiff peaks form.

Fold the egg whites into the cheese mixture. Fold in the sour cream. Place ¾ cup of the filling in a separate bowl and tint it pale green with a few drops of food coloring. Add raspberry jam to the other part and add a little pink food coloring until you achieve the desired color.

Fit a #6 tip onto a pastry bag and fill the bag with the green filling. Remove the pan from the freezer and pipe 2-inch-long vertical stripes on the inner edge of the pan. Then fill the pan with the

raspberry filling. Pipe the remaining green filling in swirls on top of the cake. Cover the pan with plastic wrap so that it doesn't touch the top of the filling and chill for at least 2 hours.

To remove the cake from the pan, soak a dish towel in hot water and wrap it around the outside of the pan just long enough to soften the butter. Then slowly release the spring on the side of the pan. Decorate with raspberry candies.

Cakes

Cakes are a very creative addition to the holiday festivities. Also, since many people have birthdays or get married during the Christmas season, having a decorative cake reflecting the colors and foliage of the season will be a special treat.

There are cake and icing recipes in the Basic Recipes section that will make all of the following designs successful, but feel free to use your favorite recipes or mixes if you wish. For the larger cakes, though, a very soft cake, such as one made from a cake mix, will not be dense enough to support the weight of the tiers and is not recommended.

For filling the cakes, you can use either the buttercream recipes given in the recipe section or your own desired fillings. I have left it up to the individual to use the filling of his or her choice since the amounts will vary in many cases. The amounts of buttercream icing in the ingredients list for each project are only for covering and decorating the cake.

Stained-Glass Cakes

PIPING GEL has been used on cakes to write "Happy Birthday" and other sentiments, or when the look of a pool of water is needed, perhaps in a fishing scene, but not for much else. The transparent quality of piping gel gave me the idea of using it to create the look of colored glass, and a Tiffany magnolia lampshade gave me the inspiration for the poinsettia design.

Piping gel can be purchased in small tubes of various colors in the grocery store baking section, or it can be bought clear from a cake-decorating supplier, tinted with liquid food coloring, and piped through a pastry bag.

Poinsettia Stained-Glass Cake

9-inch round cake, 3 inches high (2 layers)
½ recipe buttercream icing (page 144)
1 recipe rolled fondant (page 146)
12-inch cake plate
½ cup royal icing (page 145)
brown paste food coloring
pastry bags and couplers
tip #2

red, yellow, and green piping gel *or* clear piping gel and red, yellow, and green liquid food coloring
small soft paintbrush
1 yard red ½-inch-wide ribbon

Bake the cake and let it cool completely. Place any desired filling between the layers and cover the cake with a thin layer of buttercream. Cover the buttercream with rolled fondant.

Enlarge pattern 1 to 125 percent of its size. To transfer the design onto the cake, lay the pattern on the cake and prick holes with a long pin through the paper along the outlines. Keep in mind that some of the design will go over the edge and onto the side of the cake.

Tint the royal icing dark brown, fill a pastry bag with the icing, and attach the #2 tip. Outline the design with the dark-brown icing.

Next, if using clear piping gel, place about 2 heaping tablespoons of gel in each of 2 small containers. Add a few drops of the liquid coloring to each container, one red and the other green. The

gel will appear darker in the container than it will on the cake; you can test the color by spreading a little on a white surface. Add more color, a drop at a time, if necessary. Fill a pastry bag with the red piping gel, or use the tube of ready-made red gel. Fit the #2 tip onto the pastry bag.

Pipe the red petals of the poinsettia, using the illustration as a guide. Pipe a thick amount of gel at the outer tip of each petal, and then, using a paintbrush, brush the gel toward the center of the flower.

Pipe all of the green leaves in the same manner as the red petals. Add yellow piping-gel dots to the centers of the flowers. Wrap the ribbon around the bottom of the cake and pipe a dot of icing to hold it in place.

Brocade Stained Glass

9-inch round cake, 3 inches high (2 layers)
½ recipe buttercream icing (page 144)
1 recipe rolled fondant (page 146)
12-inch cake plate
½ cup royal icing (page 145)
brown paste food coloring
pastry bags and couplers
tip #2

red, yellow, green, blue, purple, and pink piping
gel *or* clear piping gel and red, yellow, green,
blue, purple, and pink liquid food coloring
1 yard ½-inch-wide red ribbon

Bake the cake and let it cool completely. Place any desired filling between the layers and cover the cake with a thin layer of buttercream. Cover the buttercream with rolled fondant.

Enlarge the pattern shapes given in pattern 2 to 125 percent of their size. To transfer the designs onto the cake, lay the patterns on the cake and prick holes with a long pin through the paper along the outlines.

Tint the royal icing dark brown, fill a pastry bag with the icing, and attach the #2 tip. Outline the designs with the dark-brown icing.

The brocade cake is decorated in the same manner as the poinsettia cake. Fill in the outlines with the different colored gels, using the photograph as a guide. Wrap the ribbon around the base of the cake and hold it in place with a dot of icing.

Floral Christmas Wreath

HOLIDAY WREATHS don't have to be red and green to say Christmas. I was inspired to create this cake by the lovely dried flower wreaths that seem to be increasingly popular. Feel free to decorate your cake with your own bouquet of royal-icing flowers. A fruitcake would be a wonderful choice for this beautiful presentation.

Serves 25

flowers and leaves in royal icing:
    10 red roses
    8 yellow roses
    15 purple chrysanthemums
    15 yellow chrysanthemums
    50 green mistletoe leaves
    20 purple statice on wires
    20 pink statice on wires
    40 white berries on toothpicks
    40 yellow baby's breath on toothpicks
red powdered food coloring
soft paintbrush
10-inch ring cake
1 recipe buttercream icing (page 144)
14-inch cake plate
yellow, pink, and red paste food coloring
pastry bags and couplers
tips #3 and #15

In advance:
    Make all of the flowers in royal icing at least one day in advance and let them dry. Dust the outer edges of the yellow mums with the red powdered coloring, using a soft paintbrush.

Flowers and Leaves in Royal Icing

Once you know the basic techniques, almost any flower can be made in icing. Royal icing dries very hard, so icing flowers can last a long time if they are kept in a covered container at room temperature and kept away from humidity. The icing should be stiff when you are piping flowers.

A flower nail is needed to make the various flowers. Use the #7 flower nail for the flowers shown. The nail is held in one hand and turned while piping with the other hand.

The basic flower nail is a long metal stick with a round, flat surface on top (fig. 1). A wax-paper square is attached to the nail with a dab of icing and the flower is piped onto the wax paper, which is then removed, along with the flower, so that you can make more flowers on the same nail.

To color flowers in royal icing, the centers or edges of the petals can be dusted with powdered food coloring with a small paintbrush to give a more realistic look. Add powders only to a completely dry flower.

Another way to vary the coloring of the flower is to paint a stripe of paste coloring inside the bag before filling it with icing. Paint the stripe along the seam of the bag to keep track of where the color is. The icing will come out of the bag in a two-colored stripe.

The directions for the flowers below list basic tip sizes. You can vary the size of the tip to get larger or smaller flowers.

Figure 1
Flower Nail

79

Figures 2–6
Making a Rose

 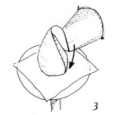   

2   3   4   5   6

The Rose

#7 flower nail
1 recipe royal icing (page 145)
red and yellow paste food coloring
2-inch squares of wax paper
pastry bags and couplers
tips #9 and #102, #103, or #104

On a sheet of wax paper, pipe large red and yellow cones with the #9 tip. Pipe as many cones as needed. Let the cones dry completely.

Place a 2-inch square of wax paper on a flower nail with a dab of icing. Attach an icing cone to the paper with a dab of icing (fig. 2). Depending on the size of the rose, fit a #102, #103, or #104 tip onto the pastry bag. Place the wide end of the tip at the base of the cone, with the narrow end facing up. Start piping around the cone, moving the tip up and then down while turning the nail counterclockwise with your other hand. Stop piping when you reach the place where you started.

You can stop here if you want only a rosebud (fig. 3), or keep going for a full bloom.

Pipe 3 petals around the bud, applying more pressure to the bag and holding the narrow end of the tip slightly away from the bud. Move the tip up and then down to form the petals (fig. 4).

Add 4 larger petals, starting and ending at the center of the previous 3 petals (fig. 5).

Add 6 larger petals around the rose to finish (fig. 6).

The Chrysanthemum

#7 flower nail
1 recipe royal icing (page 145)
purple and yellow paste food coloring
2-inch squares of wax paper
pastry bags and couplers
tip #80 or #81

Place a square of wax paper on the nail with a dab of icing. Place the #80 or #81 tip in the center of

Figures 7–10
Making a Chrysanthemum

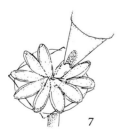   

7   8   9   10

the nail on the wax-paper square, with the rounded part of the tip against the paper. Start piping a petal out to the edge of the nail. Pipe petals all around the nail (fig. 7).

Pipe another row of petals on top of the first row (fig. 8). Pipe a third row of smaller petals on top of the second row (fig. 9). Finish the flower with very small petals in the center (fig. 10).

Mistletoe Leaves

½ recipe royal icing (page 145)
green paste food coloring
pastry bag and coupler
tip #103
wax paper

Fit a pastry bag with the #103 tip and fill the bag with green icing. On a sheet of wax paper, pipe 1½-inch-long petal-shaped leaves. Hold the tip with the narrow end facing away from you and slightly raised from the paper. Move the tip about 1 inch while applying pressure to the bag, then twist the tip a quarter of a circle (fig. 11). Finally, bring the tip down toward you, keeping the tip at a slight angle. End the leaf in a point (fig. 12). Let the leaves dry for a few hours.

Statice

2½-inch lengths of lightweight cloth-covered wire
green florist's tape
½ recipe royal icing (page 145)
green, purple, and pink paste food coloring
pastry bags and couplers
tips #4 and #13
piece of Styrofoam for drying

Hold 3 2½-inch lengths of lightweight cloth-covered wire together and wrap them with florist's tape, leaving ¾ inch uncovered at the top. Bend the uncovered wires out from the center. Using the #4 tip and green icing, insert the end of each wire into the tip and pull it out, coating the wire with icing (fig. 13). On each wire, pipe small stars with the #13 tip in purple or pink icing, covering the wire up to the taped section (fig. 14). Insert the stems in a piece of Styrofoam to dry for a few hours.

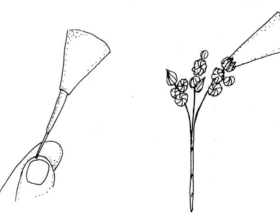

Figure 13   *Figure 14*

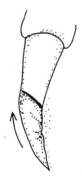
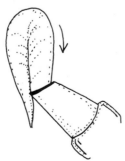

Figure 11   *Figure 12*

Berries on Toothpicks

½ recipe royal icing (page 145)
round toothpicks
green paste food coloring
pastry bags and couplers
tips #2 and #14
piece of Styrofoam for drying

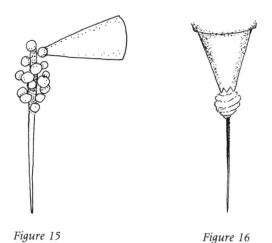

Figure 15   *Figure 16*

Fill a pastry bag with green royal icing and fit it with the #14 tip. Insert the end of a toothpick about ½ inch into the tip. Press on the bag as you pull the toothpick out, so that ½ inch of the toothpick is covered with the green icing. To dry, insert the uniced end of the toothpick in a piece of styrofoam. Pipe all of the toothpicks before proceeding. Then fit a pastry bag with a #2 tip and fill it with white royal icing. Pipe white dots on the green icing on the end of the toothpicks, allowing some of the green to show through (fig. 15). Let these dry for a few hours.

Baby's Breath on Toothpicks

½ recipe royal icing (page 145)
round toothpicks
green and yellow paste food coloring
pastry bags and couplers
tips #4 and #14
piece of Styrofoam for drying

Fill a pastry bag with green royal icing and fit it with the #4 tip. Insert a toothpick into the tip about ¾ inch to coat it with green icing. Place the other end of the toothpick in a piece of Styrofoam to dry. Finish all of the green toothpicks before continuing.

Next, pipe pale-yellow puffs of icing with the #14 tip on the ends of all of the toothpicks (fig. 16).

To decorate the cake:

Bake the cake and let it cool completely. Cover the cake with a layer of buttercream icing, making sure that you cover the inside of the ring. Starting inside the ring, place the flowers on the cake with a dot of buttercream icing piped on the bottom. Place the largest flowers first, then the smaller ones on the top and sides of the cake. Insert stemmed flowers between the other flowers, then surround them with the leaves.

When all of the flowers have been placed on the cake, prepare some salmon-colored buttercream by mixing yellow and pink coloring. Place it in a pastry bag fitted with the #15 tip. Pipe small star flowers in the spaces between the flowers. Finally, add red coloring to the remaining salmon-colored icing, and pipe red berries around the cake with the #3 tip.

The Christmas Gazebo

SINCE DECORATED BUILDINGS are a holiday tradition, I thought a gazebo festooned with garlands and wreaths would make a perfect Christmas centerpiece. But this is meant not only to be admired, but also to be eaten: it's really a cake in disguise!

Serves 130

cakes:

    11-inch round, 1½ inches high

    14-inch round, 3 inches high (2 layers)

    dome, baked in a 10-inch metal bowl, 3½
        inches high

2 recipes royal icing (page 145)

blue, green, and red paste food coloring

pastry bags and couplers

tips #2, #3, #15, #44, #199, and #352

4 ice cream cones

2 11-inch separator plates

multicolored tiny jawbreakers

8 7-inch columns

gold dragées

wax paper

white glue

vegetable shortening

16-inch round foamcore base, ⅜ inch thick

white ribbon, ⅜ inch wide

½ recipe gum paste (page 147)

10-, 11-, and 14-inch round foamcore boards

3 recipes pure white buttercream icing (page 144)

¼-inch-wide dowel rods

plastic cutting board

pizza cutter

In advance:

    Tint 1 recipe of royal icing a deep green by adding blue to green food coloring. To make the Christmas tree, stack 4 ice cream cones, making sure that together they do not exceed 6 inches high, since they will need to fit in between the 2 separator plates, which will be 7 inches apart. Using a little royal icing, attach the cones in the center of one of the separator plates, with the pegs for the columns facing up. Starting at the bottom, pipe branches with the #352 tip by attaching the icing to the cone, applying pressure to the bag, and pulling the bag away from the cone, enabling the icing to come to a point. Add the multicolored candies to the wet icing as you go up the tree. Set aside to dry.

    Next, decorate the columns. Using the green icing and the #15 tip, pipe a spiral line of icing down the length of each column (fig. 1). Tint 1 cup of the second recipe of royal icing bright red and place it in a pastry bag fitted with the #44 tip.

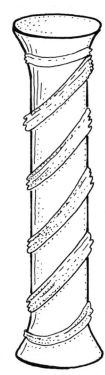

Figure 1

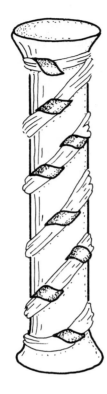

Figure 2

Fit four columns on the pegs on the bottom separator plate with the tree in the center. Glue the other four columns evenly spaced between the first four columns. Place the second separator plate on top of the columns, fitting the four pegs into the tops of four of the columns and placing a little glue on the tops of the four columns that do not have pegs.

Using the #2 tip, make the top decoration with white royal icing on wax paper, following patterns 2 and 3. Grease the wax paper *lightly* with vegetable shortening so that the decoration will not break when it is removed from the paper. Let it dry completely.

Cover the cake base with 1 cup of thinned white royal icing and let it dry completely, for about 8 hours. Glue and wrap a white ribbon around the outer edge of the board.

Make the gum paste and let it sit overnight, wrapped in plastic and placed in an airtight container.

Pipe red diagonal lines over the green spirals at 1-inch intervals, to resemble a ribbon wrapped around the garland (fig. 2). With green icing and the #2 tip, pipe needles on top of the garland by pulling the icing out to a point as you apply pressure to the bag. Pipe needles to cover the ends of the red ribbons. Add gold dragées to the wet icing.

Next, make the 15 garlands for the tops and bottoms of the columns. It's a good idea to make 15 copies of pattern 1 so you can make all of the garlands at once. Place the patterns on a cookie sheet and tape wax paper over them. With the #15 tip, pipe green lines of icing onto the paper. With the #44 tip, pipe red lines over the green lines, as you did on the columns, and then pipe the green needles and add gold dragées as above. Let these dry completely.

Pipe 8 circles for the wreaths, 1½ inches in diameter and 1 wreath 2 inches in diameter, on wax paper, in the same manner as the garlands above.

To construct the cake:

Bake all of the cakes and let them cool completely. Spread the filling of your choice on one 14-inch layer and top with the other 14-inch layer. Place each tier and the dome on its corresponding foamcore board. Cover each tier with a thin covering of buttercream icing. Let the icing dry, then cover with a thicker, smooth coat of icing. Place dowels in the 2 bottom tiers, as described in the section on tiered cakes (page 160). Place the 14-inch tier in the center of the 16-inch foamcore base. Center the smaller tier on top. Place the dome on the top separator plate and cover it with buttercream. Place the separator plates with the dome cake centered on the 2 bottom tiers.

Using the columns as a guide, make 8 marks in the top edge of the bottom tier with a toothpick. Draw a curved line between each mark with the

Place the large wreath in the center front of the dome, attaching it with a few dots of buttercream.

Attach 8 garlands to the tops of the columns with green royal icing, using the #2 tip. Attach 7 garlands between the columns, with the lowest point of the garland 1 inch from the separator plate, leaving an empty space in the front of the cake.

Using the #2 tip, pipe white royal-icing strings ⅛ inch apart from the lower garlands to the separator plate. To make the strings, attach the icing from the tip to the bottom of the garland and move the tip down to the separator plate while applying pressure to the bag. Attach the end of the line of icing to the plate. Pipe a shell border with the #15 tip to cover the bottoms of the strings.

To make the gum-paste bows, tint the gum paste red. Roll out the paste as thinly as possible onto a lightly greased cutting board. Cut ³⁄₁₆-inch-wide strips about 2 inches long with the pizza cutter. Attach 2 of them to the tops of all the wreaths, brushing a little water on the backs of the strips to make them stick. Cut more strips 1½ inches long and shape each into a loop, pinching the center together to form a bow. Attach it to the top of the wreath with a little water. Cut smaller strips about ¼ inch long and attach them to the center of each bow (figs. 8–10).

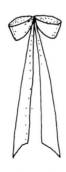
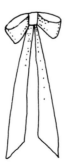

Figure 8   *Figure 9*   *Figure 10*

Christmas Quilt Cake

THE IDEA for this cake came to me after I visited a quilt museum in Pennsylvania. I converted the traditional starburst pattern into a poinsettia and used red and green as the main colors to create a Christmas motif. This would make an unusual and festive cake for a holiday wedding.

Serves 120

cakes:
> 9-inch round, 4 inches high (2 layers)
> 12-inch round, 4½ inches high (2 layers)
> 14-inch round, 4½ inches high (2 layers)

21 bamboo skewers, 4½ inches long
green liquid food coloring
3 recipes royal icing (page 145)
red, green, and yellow paste food coloring
wax paper
pastry bags and couplers
tips #1, #2, and #17
4 recipes rolled fondant (page 146)
16-inch round foamcore base, ⅜ inch thick
ruler
X-acto knife
9-, 12-, and 14-inch round foamcore boards
2 recipes buttercream icing (page 144)
rolling pin
pizza cutter
tracing wheel (found in sewing stores)
30-60-90-degree triangle
isosceles right triangle
¼-inch-wide wooden dowels
Styrofoam disk, 4 inches in diameter and 1 inch high
⅜-inch-wide white ribbon
white glue

In advance:

First, tint the bamboo skewers green, since they will serve as the stems for the flowers on top of the cake. Place the skewers in a shallow dish in which all of the sticks can lie flat. Add a few drops of liquid green food coloring to the sticks and swish them around so that all of the sticks are coated in green (if you use your hands, your fingers will turn green, too). Remove the sticks and place them on paper towels to dry.

While the sticks are drying, make the royal-icing decorations. You need to make all of these at least 2 days in advance, using patterns 1–10. Place

the patterns on a cookie sheet and tape a piece of wax paper over them. Make the decorations in the run-in sugar technique (see page 155). The 21 decorations for the top of the cake should be made on the bamboo skewers so that they can be inserted into the Styrofoam disk. Only these decorations need to be finished on both sides, because the extra layer of icing is needed to strengthen the design and lock the skewer in place. Outline and fill in one color at a time when making the decorations, since placing 2 different colors of wet icing next to each other can result in one color bleeding into the other.

Make 1 recipe of royal icing and tint it light green. Save ½ cup and tint the rest darker green. Outline the 6 large leaves on skewers, the 4 small leaves on skewers, the 4 Christmas trees, the green areas on the 8 starbursts, the mistletoe leaves for the 8 oval designs, and the 32 small green leaves (patterns 1, 4, 5, 6, 7, and 10) with the darker green icing. Thin the remaining dark-green and the reserved light-green icing and fill in the outlines. The Christmas trees only have alternating dark-green and light-green areas.

Make another recipe of royal icing and tint it red. Outline 7 hearts on skewers and 4 hearts without skewers, 4 large red flowers on skewers and 6 large red flowers without skewers, the trunks of the trees, the 8 starbursts, 32 small hearts, and the 4 small flowers (patterns 2, 3, 5, 6, 8, and 9). Save about ¼ cup of the icing and thin the rest. Fill in the red flowers, the trunks of the trees, 4 of the starbursts, and the small hearts, then pipe small dots for the 8 oval designs.

Make another recipe of royal icing. Thin about 1½ cups and fill in all of the large hearts and the other 4 starbursts with white icing. When the icing is dry, pipe small red dots with the #1 tip on the white hearts.

Finish the backs of the skewered designs with another coat of icing.

Tint about ½ cup of the white icing yellow and pipe dots on the trees, the centers of the red flowers, and a line on the large leaves.

Outline the inner star with white icing with the #2 tip in the center of the 4 red starbursts.

Make the rolled fondant, wrap it with plastic wrap, and store it in an airtight container for at least 8 hours.

Cover the 16-inch base with 1 cup of thinned white royal icing.

To decorate the cakes:

Bake the cakes and let them cool completely. Since there are no octagonal-shaped cake pans, you will need to cut the cakes into octagons yourself. To make templates for the octagons, outline the bottom of each pan on a sheet of paper and cut it out. Fold each circle in half, then into quarters, then into eighths. Place a ruler across the 2 points on the paper that make the ends of the arc (fig. 1) and cut off the rounded part. When you open the paper, you will have an octagon. Lay each pattern piece flat on the corresponding foamcore board and cut out the octagon, using an X-acto knife and ruler. The foamcore octagons will be the bases for each tier.

Spread the cake layers with your desired filling and stack the 2 layers of each size to form 3 tiers. Place the appropriate paper pattern on top of each tier and cut the cake vertically to form octagons. Place each tier on its corresponding foamcore base.

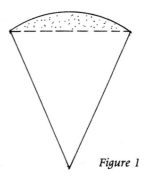

Figure 1

Measure each tier to make sure it is the correct height. Trim the cake horizontally if the cake is too high, using a serrated knife. Cover each tier with a thin coat of buttercream icing to set the crumbs and to allow the fondant to adhere to the sides of the cake.

To do the quilting on the fondant, you will need a tracing wheel and 2 triangles. You must cover and quilt one tier at a time; if the fondant is left to be quilted later, it will crack. Roll out the fondant as directed in the section on rolled fondant (page 146) and cover a tier, smoothing the top and then the sides and trimming off the excess.

Each tier is quilted in a different manner. The 9-inch tier is quilted with diagonal lines, with each side slanting in the opposite direction from the one before. To make the quilt lines, place the 30-60-90-degree triangle flat on the table, with the hypotenuse against the cake (the 30-degree angle should be facing up) at one corner of the section you plan to quilt. Place the tracing wheel against the triangle and emboss a dotted line into the fon-

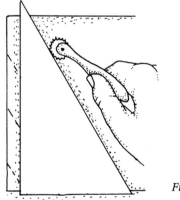

Figure 2

dant as you roll it down the edge (fig. 2). Each of the 8 sections should have 8 diagonal lines, equally spaced, and facing in a different direction on each side (fig. 3).

For the 12-inch tier, each side of the octagon needs to be divided into 4 equal sections. Each side should measure 4½ inches high by 4½ inches wide. Find the center of each side with a ruler and lightly mark a horizontal and vertical cross in the

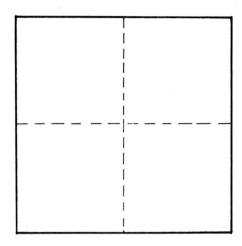

Figure 4

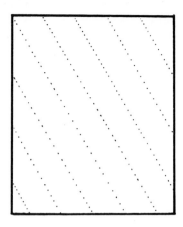

Figure 3

center of the square, using the tracing wheel to make the lines (fig. 4). Divide the horizontal line into ½-inch segments. Then divide the top edge into ½-inch segments, starting at the center line. These marks will be indications as to where to draw the diagonal lines. The diagonal lines slant down from right to left in the upper left- and lower right-hand corners. The lines slant from left to right in the opposite corners. Place the isosceles right triangle flat on the table with the hypotenuse against the cake. Emboss diagonal lines with your tracing wheel, using the ½-inch marks as a guide.

Stop embossing when you reach the center line. Emboss all of the lines going in one direction, then turn the triangle around and emboss the lines in the other direction. When you are finished, you will have an embossed diamond shape (fig. 5).

The quilting on the 14-inch tier consists of diagonal squares. Each side should measure 5½ inches wide. Using a ruler, measure 1⅛-inch intervals across the top edge of each side. These are the marks on which you will start embossing the diagonal lines. Lay the isosceles right triangle flat on the table and emboss all of the lines slanting up

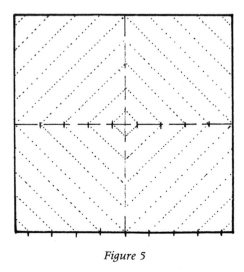

Figure 5

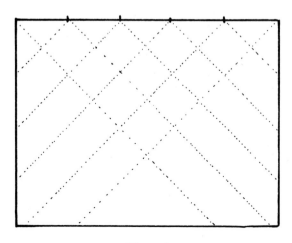

Figure 6

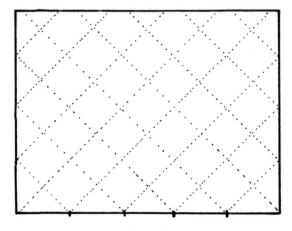

Figure 7

from right to left, then emboss the lines slanting up from left to right, using the marks as a guide (fig. 6). The points where the lines meet the side of the section mark the beginning of the rest of the diagonal lines (fig. 7).

When all of the embossed quilt lines have been made, insert the dowels in each tier as directed in the section on tiered cakes (page 160). Stack the

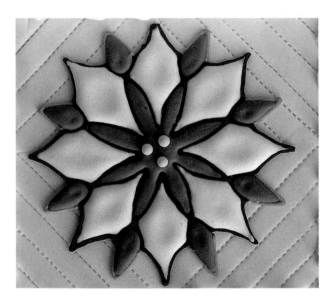

cakes, first placing the bottom tier on the 16-inch base with a little buttercream icing to hold it in place. The 12-inch tier is placed on top of the 14-inch tier so that the corners of the 8 segments of the smaller tier line up with the centers of the segments on the larger one. The 9-inch tier is lined up to the 12-inch tier in the same way.

Attach the royal-icing appliqués to the segments on the tiers with a little buttercream icing, using the photograph as a guide. Place the 32 small red hearts on the tops of each tier in the corners of each section and on the base. Connect the leaves on the oval design and on the top-tier flowers with dotted lines of green icing, using the #2 tip.

To make the top ornament, cut a piece of wax paper the same size as the bottom of the Styrofoam disk and glue it to the bottom of the disk with a dab of royal icing. Cover the disk with rolled fondant. Insert the royal-icing decorations on skewers into the disk, starting at the top center with a large heart. Then insert 4 of the red flowers around and slightly below the top heart. Insert the 4 small leaves between the red flowers. Next, insert the remaining 6 hearts around and below the leaves. Then insert the 6 large leaves in between the hearts at an angle. You may have to cut down the skewers as you go if they are too long. Place the top ornament on the top of the cake, using a dab of icing to hold it in place. Pipe a buttercream shell border around the bottom edge of the disk, using the #17 tip. Add the 6 red flowers around the edge of the disk, securing them with a dot of buttercream behind each one.

Finally, pipe a shell border with the #17 tip, using white buttercream icing, along all of the edges of the cake, including the divisions between the sections on each tier.

Glue the white ribbon around the edge of the base.

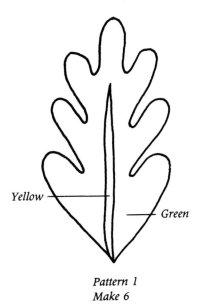

Yellow

Green

Pattern 1
Make 6

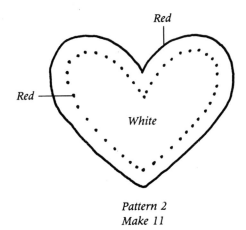

Red

Red

White

Pattern 2
Make 11

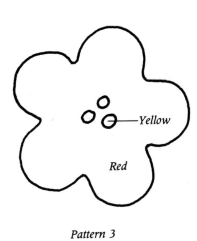

Yellow

Red

Pattern 3
Make 10

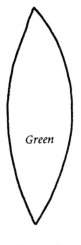

Green

Pattern 4
Make 4

Snowflake Wedding Cake

To DECORATE a winter wedding cake, snowflakes are a beautiful alternative to flowers. Because the snowflakes are quite delicate, I recommend using royal icing made with egg whites rather than meringue powder.

I tried a new product on this cake — food coloring in a spray can, which gives the cake a delicate coloration. If you cannot find this product, you can achieve similar results by slightly kneading the rolled fondant with a little blue paste food coloring for a marbleized effect.

Serves 85

cakes:

   6-inch petal-shaped, 4 inches high (2 layers)
   9-inch petal-shaped, 4 inches high (2 layers)
   15-inch petal-shaped, 4 inches high (2 layers)
2 recipes royal icing (page 145), made with egg whites instead of meringue powder
wax paper
vegetable shortening
cookie sheets
pastry bag and coupler
tips #2 and #15
edible glitter
20 white, heavy-gauge, cloth-covered wires, 6 inches long
2 tart pans, 1½ and 2 inches across on the bottom
2 sugar molds, made in tart pans, 3 inches and 2½ inches wide at the top (see page 156)
4 recipes rolled fondant (page 146)
19-inch round foamcore board, ⅜ inch thick
6-, 9-, and 15-inch petal-shaped foamcore boards
1 recipe buttercream icing (page 144)
rolling pin
pizza cutter

1 can blue Creative Color Decorating Food Spray *or* blue paste food coloring
large and small silver dragées
¼-inch-wide wooden dowels
white glue
5 yards ⅜-inch-wide white ribbon
Styrofoam ball, 2 inches in diameter

In advance:

   Make 50 snowflakes of various sizes on wax paper. It is a good idea to coat the paper first with a little shortening; this will make removing the snowflakes easier. *Do not* use vegetable spray, such as Pam. A thick coating of oil will break down the royal icing. Place patterns 1–6 on a cookie sheet, cover them with wax paper, and tape down the edges to hold it in place. Pipe royal icing with the

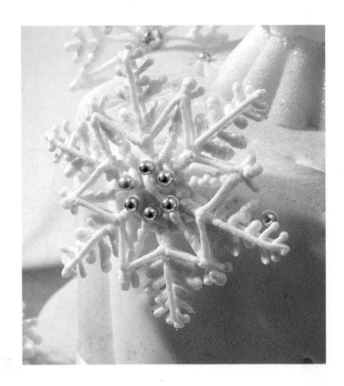

#2 tip, either following the patterns or designing your own six-sided variations. While the icing is still wet, sprinkle with edible glitter. Make about 30 snowflakes.

Next you need to make 20 snowflakes on wires. Place a wire over each pattern so that one end is in the center of the snowflake. Pipe the snowflake over the wire, sprinkle with glitter, and let dry. Carefully turn the snowflake over and repipe the back to reinforce the icing.

Pipe a simple snowflake pattern on the back of each of the 2 tart pans with royal icing (patterns 7 and 8). Let dry. These will serve as tools for embossing in the rolled fondant.

Make the sugar molds according to the directions in the section on sugar molds (page 156).

Make the rolled fondant, wrap it in plastic wrap, and store it in an airtight container.

Cover the foamcore base with 1 cup of thinned white royal icing. Let it dry for 24 hours.

To decorate the cakes:

Bake all of the cakes and cool them completely. Place each bottom layer on its corresponding foamcore board, using a dab of icing to hold it in place. (If you cannot find petal-shaped boards, you can make them out of foamcore, using the bottom of each cake pan as a pattern.) Spread your desired filling on the bottom layer, then add the top layer. Cover each tier with a thin coating of buttercream icing, then cover with rolled fondant. (If you do not have the spray coloring, knead a little blue paste coloring into the fondant before you place it on the cake.)

After you cover each tier, press the icing design on the back of the tart pans into the fondant to emboss it. Alternate large and small snowflakes around the cake in a random pattern.

Spray the cake lightly with a little of the food coloring (test the spray first on a piece of paper).

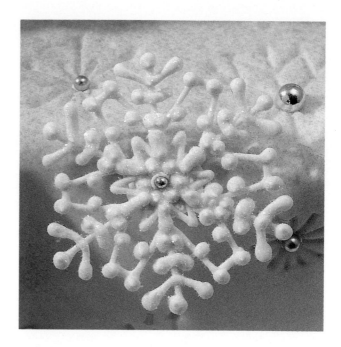

Place large and small dragées in the centers of the embossed designs, using dots of royal icing to hold them in place.

Add the dowels to each tier and stack the cakes on the base according to the directions in the section on tiered cakes (page 160).

Attach ribbon to the edge of the base with glue and to the bottom of each tier with a little royal icing.

Glue the Styrofoam ball in the hollow of the 3-inch sugar mold with royal icing. Attach the other mold upside down to the bottom of the first mold with a little royal icing. Start inserting the wired snowflakes into the Styrofoam ball, piping icing around the bottoms of the wires with the #15 tip, until the whole ball is covered. Be very careful not to bump the snowflakes, or they will break.

Attach the remaining snowflakes to the cake with a little royal icing. Attach the snowflake bouquet on the top.

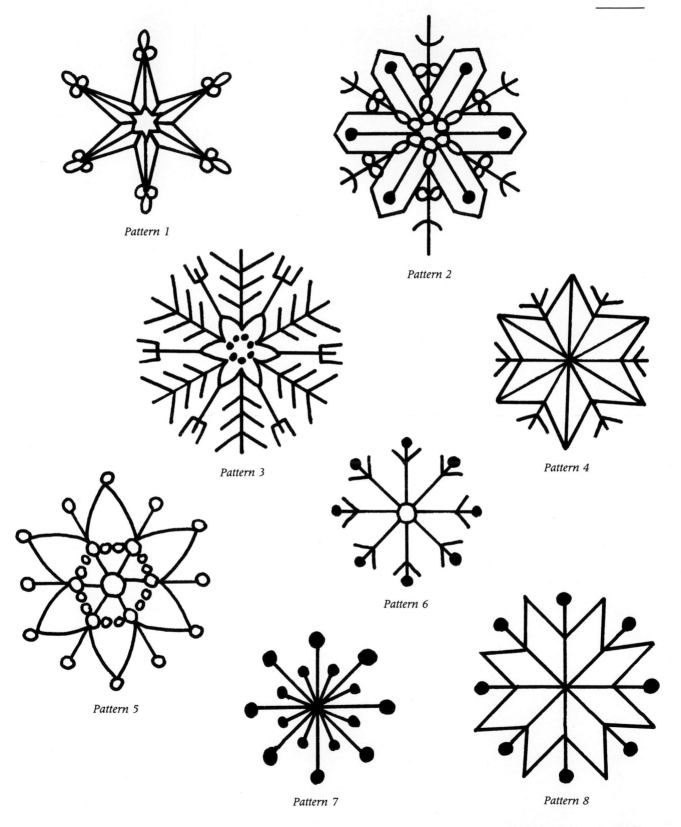

Pattern 1

Pattern 2

Pattern 3

Pattern 4

Pattern 5

Pattern 6

Pattern 7

Pattern 8

Golden Fantasy Wedding Cake

ROLLED FONDANT is gathered and draped to give the look of fabric on this elegant cake. The gold stars add a touch of magic to your holiday celebration.

Serves 120

cakes:

    6-inch round, 3½ inches high (2 layers)
    8-inch round, 4 inches high (2 layers)
    10-inch round, 4½ inches high (2 layers)
    12-inch round, 6 inches high (3 layers)
2 recipes royal icing (page 145)
wax paper
2 or more cookie sheets
pastry bag and coupler
tips #2 and #17
30 white, heavy-gauge, cloth-covered wires, 6
    inches long
small paintbrush
nontoxic gold powder
lemon extract
piece of Styrofoam for drying stars
6 recipes rolled fondant (page 146)
14-inch round foamcore base, ⅜ inch thick
gold decorative foil
masking tape
6-, 8-, 10-, and 12-inch round foamcore boards
2 7-inch separator plates
2 recipes buttercream icing (page 144)
cornstarch
rolling pin
pizza cutter
¼-inch-wide wooden dowels
4 gold columns, 3 inches high
18-inch ruler
tape measure
5 yards ⅜-inch-wide white ribbon
Styrofoam ball, 3 inches in diameter, cut in half

In advance:

You will need 70 royal-icing stars, 20 of which will be made on wires. Use the pattern shapes given in pattern 1 and make roughly equal numbers of all of the sizes. Place the patterns under a sheet of wax paper and tape the paper to a cookie sheet. Pipe outlines of the stars on the wax paper with white royal icing and the #2 tip. For the stars on wires, place the end of a wire in the center of an outlined star. Thin the royal icing with a few drops of water until it is the consistency of thick corn syrup. Fill in the outlines with the thinned icing, using the #2 tip. (See the section on run-in sugar, page 155.) Let these dry completely for 24 hours. Then turn the wired stars over and fill in the backs with thinned icing, using a small paintbrush to brush the icing to the edges. (The stars on wires need to be reinforced on the back with more icing to ensure that the wire is firmly attached.) Let these stars dry for another 8 hours.

When all of the stars are dry, paint them with a mixture of nontoxic gold powder and lemon extract, using a 2-to-1 ratio of extract to powder. I usually start with about ⅛ teaspoon of the gold and add ¼ teaspoon extract. If the mixture streaks, it can be thickened with a little gold powder. If it is too thick, add a drop or two of the extract. Because of its high alcohol content, the extract tends to evaporate quickly, so you may have to add a drop or two while you are working. (*Hint:* When you are finished painting, let the mixture stand until the extract evaporates; the gold powder that remains can be reused.) Paint both the fronts and backs of the wired stars. Insert the ends of the wires in a piece of Styrofoam to dry. Paint only the fronts of the other stars. Let them all dry thoroughly.

Wrap the 10 remaining wires tightly around a pencil to form corkscrew curls. Pull the pencil out, then pull on each end of the wire to elongate it. Paint all of the corkscrews and the wires with the stars with the gold mixture and let them dry.

Make the rolled fondant. Wrap it in plastic and store it in an airtight container 24 hours in advance.

Cover the base with decorative foil, taping it to the bottom with masking tape.

To decorate the cake:

Bake all of the cakes and let them cool completely. Using a dab of icing to hold the cake in place, set the bottom layer of each tier on its corresponding foamcore base and then place the 6-inch tier on one of the 7-inch separator plates. Spread your desired filling on the bottom layer and then add the next layer (repeat for the third layer of the 12-inch tier). Cover each tier with a thin layer of buttercream icing, then cover each with a *thin* layer of rolled fondant. The rolled fondant layer is necessary because the draped fondant that will cover it is heavy and will need a sturdy base to adhere to.

Place dowels in the tiers as directed in the section on tiered cakes (page 160). Stack the three larger tiers with a little buttercream icing between them to hold them in place. Place the columns on the pegs of the bottom separator plate and attach the plate holding the top tier to the tops of the columns.

To make the rolled fondant "skirt," start at the top of the cake. Roll out a piece of fondant on a surface lightly coated with cornstarch, approximately 3/16 inch thick, or as thin as you can roll it and still handle it without tearing. With the pizza cutter, cut a strip about 18 inches long and about 1/2 inch wider than the height of the tier. Turn the strip over and brush both of the long edges with a little water to make the fondant slightly sticky. (For the bottom tier, the fondant is brushed only on the top, since the bottom of the "skirt" just

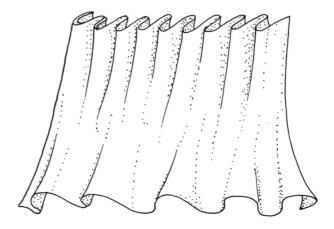

Figure 1

hangs and is not attached to the cake.) Gently gather the strip lengthwise from one end to the other, in an accordion fold (fig. 1). Press the fondant to the top of the cake and slightly flatten the top edge of the draped piece. Press the bottom of the fondant to the bottom of the tier. Cut and attach strips of fondant to the cake one at a time, so that the icing does not dry out and crack. When attaching a second strip next to the first, fold over the edge that overlaps the first strip, so that the fondant appears to be continuous. Repeat as many times as needed to drape the entire tier, then do the same for the other tiers.

For the swags, carefully measure the circumference of the top of each tier with a tape measure. The bottom tier has 6 swags, while the other 2 tiers have 5 apiece. Fold the measured length on the tape measure into 5 or 6 equal sections, depending on which tier you are decorating. This will tell you how long to cut the strips, which should be 3 inches wide. Brush the two short edges of the back of each strip with a little water and gently gather both ends of the fondant and place on the top edge of the cake, letting the middle of the strip drape downward. This should cover the top of the fondant skirt. Repeat until the top of each tier is completely covered.

To make each vertical sash, cut the fondant according to pattern 2, and brush one end with water. Gently place the sash between the ends of two swags.

Wrap white ribbon around the bottom of each tier and secure the ends with a dot of royal icing.

Next, cut the Styrofoam ball in half with a serrated knife. Sand the bottom of one half with the other half until it is smooth. Cut out a circle of wax paper the same size as the bottom of the Styrofoam ball. Place a dab of royal icing on the wax paper and press on the bottom of the ball. Starting at the top, insert stars and some corkscrew curls into the ball, using different sizes of stars and lengths of wire for variety. As you work, pipe royal icing with the #17 tip around the bottoms of the wires to hold them in place. Let this dry for 24 hours.

To place the unwired stars on the cake, pipe dots of royal icing on the backs and place them randomly around the cake. Insert the remaining corkscrew curls here and there.

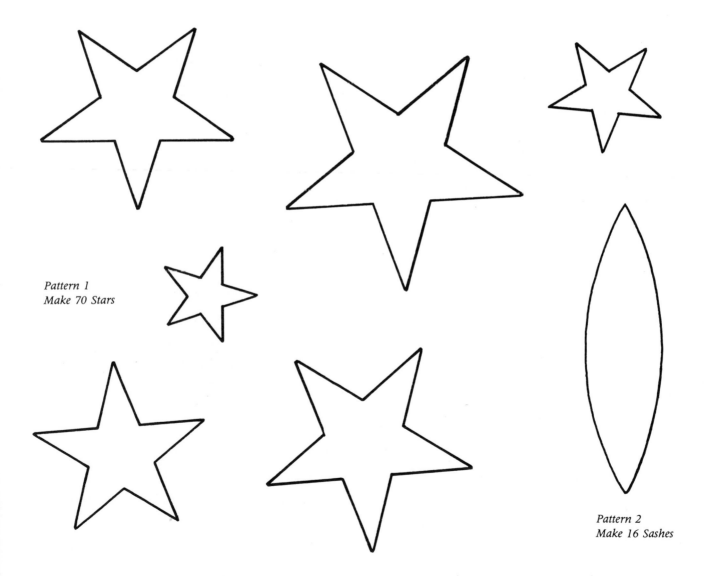

Pattern 1
Make 70 Stars

Pattern 2
Make 16 Sashes

Christmas Presents

CHRISTMAS PRESENTS are a natural motif for Christmas cake. Each tier can be decorated in an unlimited variety of colors and designs, and bows of many colors top each tier.

Serves 170

cakes:

    6-inch square, 3 inches high (2 layers)

    10-inch square, 3½ inches high (2 layers)

    14-inch square, 4½ inches high (2 layers)

4 recipes royal icing (page 145)

wax paper

cookie sheets

red, green, brown, and yellow paste food coloring

pastry bags and couplers

tips #1, #2, #3, #4, #7, #13, #16, #18, #30, #46, #48, #59, and #61

18-inch square foamcore base, ⅜ inch thick

4 recipes buttercream icing (page 144)

6-, 10-, and 14-inch square foamcore boards

¼-inch-wide wooden dowels

⅜-inch-wide white ribbon

In advance:

The three small packages on the top of the cake, the bows, and all of the appliqué designs are made from royal icing and should be made at least 2 days in advance. The royal-icing designs are all made on wax paper on a cookie sheet with the necessary patterns taped underneath. Make 1 recipe of royal icing at a time, and make all of the designs in one color at the same time.

Make 1 recipe of royal icing and tint it a pale butterscotch color, using brown and yellow coloring. Using the #2 tip, outline the box patterns (patterns 1–6) in the numbers given. Then thin 1½ cups of the tinted icing as directed in the sec-

tion on run-in sugar (page 155) and fill in the outlines using the #2 tip. Let these dry completely. Save the remaining icing for constructing the boxes.

Tint another recipe of royal icing red. Pipe 25 2½-inch-long loops, using the #30 tip for the large bow. Then pipe 25 smaller loops with the #59 tip for the smaller red bow (see the section on royal-icing bows, page 156). Using patterns 7–9, outline the poinsettia petals with the #2 tip in the numbers specified. Pipe 5 red vertical lines on the 4 sides and the top of box patterns 2 and 3, using the #3 tip. Thin the remaining icing and fill in the outlines of the petals using the #2 tip.

Make another recipe of royal icing and tint 1 cup yellow. Save the remaining white icing for later. Pipe 25 ¾-inch-long loops with the #46 tip for the small yellow bow. Using the #3 tip, pipe 8 yellow horizontal lines over the red lines on the plaid box pieces. Save the rest of the yellow icing for constructing the bow.

Make another recipe of royal icing. Tint it light green, remove 1 cup, and tint the other 1½ cups darker green. Pipe 30 dark-green loops with the #61 tip on wax paper. Using patterns 10 and 11, outline the poinsettia leaves with royal icing from the #2 tip on wax paper, making 15 of the leaves in light green and 25 in dark green. Outline the holly and mistletoe patterns (patterns 12 and 13) in the 2 shades of green. Pipe 4 green vertical lines on the plaid box pieces, using the #4 tip. After the box is constructed, finish the corners with another green vertical line. Thin the icing and fill in all of the outlined leaves in the 2 shades of green.

When all of the box pieces have dried, they can be glued together with royal icing. With the remaining butterscotch icing and the #16 tip, construct the boxes in the same manner as the Cookie Gift Boxes (see page 40). Let the boxes dry completely before adding decorations.

To decorate the larger mistletoe box, attach the leaves with dots of icing, as indicated in the photograph. Pipe white dots around the leaves with the #3 tip. Construct the small red bow on the top of the box, as directed in the section on royal-icing bows (page 156).

Construct the yellow bow on the plaid box.

To decorate the small candy-cane box use the #13 tip and pipe small white candy canes randomly around the 4 sides and the top of the box. Piping candy canes is similar to piping a shell, except that the tail of the shell is elongated (fig. 1). Then tint ¼ cup of the remaining white icing red and, with the #1 tip, pipe stripes on each cane, following the grooves in the white icing (fig. 2). Pipe green dots around the candy canes with the #3 tip.

Cover the 18-inch base with thinned butterscotch-colored royal icing and let it dry for 24 hours.

Figure 1   *Figure 2*

To decorate the cake:

Bake all of the cakes and cool them completely. Make the buttercream icing and tint 3 of the recipes the same butterscotch color as before. (*Hint:* Tinted buttercream icing gets darker as it sets, so make the colors a shade lighter than you want.) For the fourth recipe, tint 2½ cups red, 2 cups white, 1 cup green, and ½ cup yellow.

Place the bottom layers on their corresponding foamcore boards, spread your desired filling on the layers, and place the top layers over the filling. Cover the cakes with 2 layers of butterscotch-colored buttercream icing.

The tiers are not stacked directly on top of each other. The 10-inch tier should be positioned 1 inch from the back and left side of the 14-inch tier, and the 6-inch tier should be 1 inch from the back and right side of the 10-inch tier. Mark the placement of each tier on the cake below and place dowels in the tiers according to the directions for tiered cakes (page 160). Stack the tiers on the base.

Starting with the bottom tier, attach the poinsettia petals as indicated in the photograph, with the smaller petals in the center. Use dots of buttercream icing to hold them in place. Then pipe 5 or 6 green dots in the center of each flower with the #2 tip. Pipe tiny dots of red with the #1 tip on the end of each dot. Attach leaves around the flowers. Pipe yellow veins on some of the leaves, using the #2 tip. Pipe a shell border around the base of the tier with the #30 tip, using butterscotch-colored buttercream.

On the next tier, pipe 7 evenly spaced red vertical buttercream stripes on each side, using the #48 tip. Pipe a green stripe on either side of the red stripe with the #7 tip. Pipe a white zigzag stripe with the #16 tip between the red stripes, then pipe small red dots along every other white stripe with the #2 tip. Pipe a butterscotch border with the #30 tip around the base of the tier. All of the piping is in buttercream icing.

Construct the large red bow in the right front corner of the bottom tier with red royal icing.

To decorate the 6-inch tier, pipe squiggles all over the surface with the #2 tip and yellow buttercream icing. Place the holly leaves on the cake with dots of icing, then pipe small red dots with the #2 tip around the leaves. Pipe a butterscotch-colored buttercream shell border around the bottom edge with the #18 tip. Construct the green bow with green royal icing on the front left corner of the 10-inch tier.

Attach the royal-icing packages to the top of the cake with dots of buttercream icing.

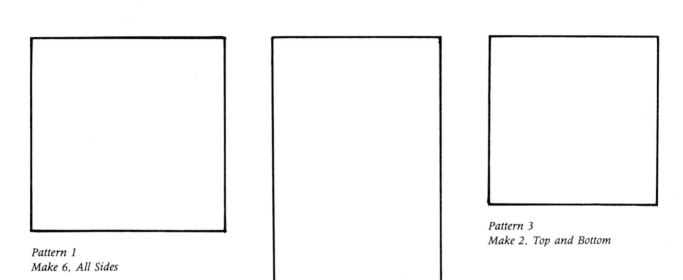

Pattern 1
Make 6, All Sides

Pattern 2
Make 4, Sides

Pattern 3
Make 2, Top and Bottom

Pattern 4
Make 2, Front and Back

Pattern 6
Make 2, Top and Bottom

Pattern 5
Make 2, Sides

Pattern 7
Make 72

Pattern 8
Make 40

Pattern 9
Make 48

Pattern 10
Make 25

Pattern 11
Make 15

Pattern 12
Make 35

Pattern 13
Make 50

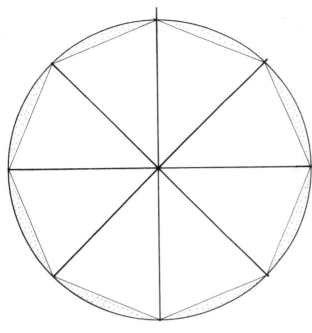

Figure 8

inches in diameter on a piece of paper and cut it out. Fold the circle in half, then into quarters, then into eighths. Trim off the arcs to form an octagon (fig. 8). Trace the outline of the octagon on the 8½-inch piece of foamcore. Cut out the shape with an X-acto knife and ruler. Make another foamcore octagon in the same way as above, starting with a 2¾-inch circle. Next, cut out a 3¾-inch circle of foamcore. Glue the smaller foamcore octagon in the center of the foamcore circle.

Sharpen both ends of the ⁵⁄₁₆-inch-wide dowels, ¼ inch from each end (like a two-ended pencil). Using a sharpened dowel, make holes in one side of the large octagon at 7 of the 8 corners, ¼ inch in from the outer edge. Make similar holes in the top of the smaller octagon.

Cut out 8 foamcore triangles using pattern 5. Bevel each side of each triangle with the X-acto knife, laying the triangle flat on a cutting board and holding the blade at a 45-degree angle (fig.

9). Using wood glue, attach the short side of a triangle, beveled edge down, to the top edge of the large octagon (the side without the holes). Put glue along each side of the triangle and on the adjacent edges of the large triangle, then glue another triangle to each side of the first one. Repeat with the remaining 5 triangles (fig. 10). Tape them together with a little masking tape until the glue is dry. Cut off the top about ¼ inch down to flatten it. When the glue is dry, cover the surface of the 8 triangles with a thin, smooth layer of royal icing.

Next, place glue in the holes on the small octagon and insert the 7 dowels. Place glue on the tips of the dowels and insert them into the holes on the underside of the large octagon. Rearrange the dowels if necessary so that all of them are evenly slanted (fig. 11). Let the glue dry overnight.

Glue the wide ends of the sugar molds together with royal icing. Let the icing set for about an hour, then glue them onto the cone-shaped top of the cage with royal icing. Attach the gum-paste ball to the top of the sugar molds with icing and let it dry.

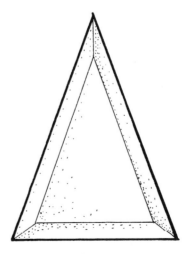

Figure 9

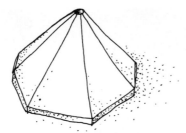

Figure 10

Roll two cylinders of gum paste, each ⅛ inch wide and about 16 inches long. Twist them together to form a rope. Brush a little water on the back of the rope and press it around the outer edge of the octagon on the roof of the birdcage. Pipe a line of icing with the #4 tip along the 8 seams on the roof. Pipe a border of dots alongside each line, then overpipe another line on top of the first one. Pipe a dot at the end of each line.

Using icing, glue half of a 2-inch Styrofoam ball in the center of the base of the birdcage, then glue the other half onto the center of a separator plate with the pegs facing up. Let the icing and the gum paste dry overnight. Paint the entire surface of the cage (except the Styrofoam ball) with the gold mixture and let it dry.

To decorate the columns, cut out 6 strips of gum paste approximately ⅜ inch wide and 8 inches long. Moisten the back of each strip with a little water and gently press it onto a column, spiraling downward. Let the gum paste dry, then paint it with the gold mixture.

To make the 16 ropes and tassels, place patterns 6 and 7 on a cookie sheet and tape a piece of wax paper over them. Using tip #15, pipe royal-icing ropes with a circular motion. Make 8 of each size. With the #2 tip, pipe the tassels on the end of the ropes, using a circular motion (fig. 12). Pipe 5 horizontal lines with the #2 tip at the top of each tassel (see the patterns). Let them dry overnight, then paint them with the gold mixture.

Cover the base with 1½ cups of thinned white royal icing and let it dry for 24 hours. Glue the white ribbon around the edge of the board.

Make the rolled fondant, wrap it in plastic, and place it in an airtight container overnight.

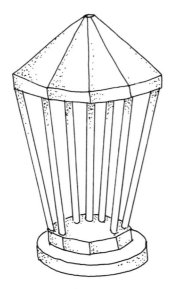

Figure 11

Figure 12

To decorate the cake:

Bake all of the cakes and let them cool completely. Place each level on its corresponding masonite board, holding it in place with a dab of icing. Spread your desired filling on the bottom layer and add the top layer. Cover the two with buttercream, then cover with fondant. Attach the bottom tier to the separator plate with a dab of buttercream. Insert the gumpaste dowels in the top tier to support the table above, being careful to

Ornaments and Decorations

When my sister Doreen and I were children, we spent hours making ornaments out of Styrofoam balls and ribbon. Every Christmas my mother still decorates the house with those ornaments. Here are some edible ornaments and decorations that taste as good as they look. They are fun to make and will keep the kids — and the adults — busy for hours.

Chocolate Almond Pine Cones

THESE PINE CONES are deliciously simple. They look festive arranged like a wreath on a platter, and kids will have fun dipping them in the chocolate glaze.

Makes about 20 pine cones

14 ounces marzipan
8 ounces whole almonds
1 recipe chocolate glaze (see recipe below)
optional: ½ cup dark-green royal icing (page
    145); wax paper; pastry bag and coupler;
    tip #4

To make the pine cones:

Using a small, sharp knife, cut the almonds in half lengthwise along the seam. Form a cone of marzipan about 1 to 1¼ inches wide at the base and about 1½ to 2 inches high. Place an almond half with the pointed end down in the top of the marzipan cone. Continue inserting the almonds with the rounded halves facing out around the cone, staggering the rows as shown in the photograph. Fill in the entire cone and carefully set it aside. Repeat, making pine cones in slightly different sizes for variety.

To make the chocolate glaze:
1½ cups (12 ounces) heavy cream
12 ounces semisweet chocolate chips
1 tablespoon Grand Marnier or amaretto liqueur

Place the cream in a heavy saucepan and heat until it just reaches the boiling point. Remove the pan from the heat and add the chocolate chips. Cover the pan for 10 minutes, stir, and add the liqueur. The mixture will become smooth and shiny. Use the glaze immediately; as the glaze cools, it becomes stiff. (The glaze can be refrigerated for 2 weeks. Reheat over low heat, stirring constantly, until it reaches a pourable consistency. You can also reheat it in the microwave on low for a few minutes, stirring occasionally.)

To dip the pine cones in the glaze, place a rack over a sheet pan or cookie sheet. Press a fork into the bottom of the pine cone and dip the cone into the chocolate, turning it carefully so you do not disturb the almonds. Coat the entire cone with chocolate. With another fork, gently slide the cone off the first fork and place it upright on the rack over the cookie sheet. The excess glaze will drip onto the sheet and can be reused.

Refrigerate the pine cones just long enough for the chocolate to set, about 5 minutes. Longer refrigeration will dull the shine of the chocolate. Arrange the cones on a platter in a wreath formation. They can be kept at room temperature for 2 days, but they probably won't last that long!

If you wish, you can pipe pine needles to decorate the platter. With the #4 tip and dark-green royal icing, pipe lines about 2 inches long on wax paper and let them dry for a few hours. Place them around the pine cones on the platter.

Molded Sugar Ornaments

THESE ORNAMENTS are made completely from sugar and edible decorations. They look wonderful on the tree and will last for a few Christmases if kept in a cool, dry place.

sugar molds made from ball molds, tart pans, or
    bell molds (page 156)
1 recipe royal icing (page 145)
X-acto knife
colored ribbons
large and small silver and gold dragées
small paintbrush
clear and colored piping gel
colored edible glitter
colored sugar
pastry bag and coupler
tips #2 and #44

Make the sugar molds and hollow them out according to the directions in the section on sugar molds. The bell ornaments are made in one piece, while the ball and the tart-pan ornaments are made in 2 halves, glued together with royal icing, and then decorated. Before gluing the 2 halves together, take a length of ribbon 9 inches long, tie the 2 ends in a knot, and glue the knotted end with royal icing inside one half of the mold. Pipe some royal icing on the inside edge of the mold, then press the other half of the mold against the icing. Let dry for a few hours. Cover the seam with piped royal icing, dragées, or colored sugar.

To place the ribbon in the bell mold, use an X-acto knife and make a small hole in the top of the mold, using a drilling motion. Then push the knotted ribbon up through the hole from the bottom of the bell. The knot will hold the ribbon in place.

Purple Ball with Gold and Silver Dragées

Glue 12 gold dragées in a circle on the side of the ball, using royal icing and the #2 tip. Keep making circles, with each circle touching the one next to it (fig. 1), until the whole surface is covered. Now glue large silver dragées in the spaces between the circles. When the icing is dry, brush clear piping gel in the middle of each circle and sprinkle purple glitter on the gel. Let dry for 24 hours.

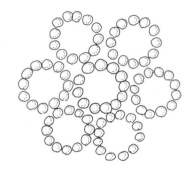

Figure 1

Bell with Silver and Gold Dragées

To make the bell ornament, place the mold on a piece of wax paper and glue large silver dragées around the base of the bell with royal icing and the #2 tip. Glue gold dragées on top and in between each silver dragée. Continue gluing on dragées, using the photograph as a guide.

Gold and Silver Star Ornament

For the star ornament, make 2 3-inch tart-pan molds. When you glue the 2 halves together, do not line up the scallops on the sides of the mold. Instead, stagger the scallops (fig. 2). Then glue large silver dragées to both sides of the flat part of each scallop. Glue dragées using the photograph as a guide. Pipe a dot border around the seam of the two molds with royal icing and the #2 tip.

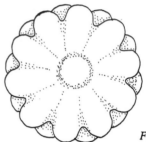

Figure 2

Colored-Sugar Bells, Balls, and Stars

Make the appropriate shaped molds and paint on the designs, stripes, and so on with clear or colored piping gel. Then sprinkle colored sugar, glitter, or tiny dragées in the gel. Use one color at a time so that the colored sugars and glitters do not mix on the gel. Pipe gel to outline the designs and place dragées in the gel. Use the photograph as a guide for the various designs.

White Latticework Ball

Using the #44 tip and white icing, pipe parallel lines, following the contours of the ball (fig. 3). Space the lines about ¾ inch apart. Then pipe lines going in the opposite direction (fig. 4). Attach a gold dragée at each intersection of the lines. Glue 6 small silver dragées in a circle around each gold dragée.

Figure 3

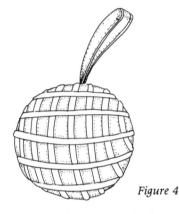

Figure 4

Mosaic Candy Tree

I HAVE ALWAYS loved mosaics, so I thought it would be fun to make a Christmas tree that was a candy mosaic. The kids will love helping with this colorful centerpiece and eating the leftovers, too.

string
pushpin
28-inch-square foamcore board
18-inch metal ruler
X-acto knife
white glue
masking tape
10-inch circle of foamcore
25-inch-long cardboard tube from roll of
    wrapping paper
2 recipes royal icing (page 145)
pastry bag and coupler
tips #3 and #16
2 stacks of books
assorted candies such as:
    14 8-inch candy sticks
    103 spearmint leaves
    1 pound miniature jawbreakers
    30 blue jelly beans
    182 pink jelly beans
    50 white jelly beans
    34 peach jelly beans
    16 yellow jelly beans
    10 purple jelly beans
    62 kernels green and yellow Indian Corn
    32 red Chiclets
    4 green Chiclets
    46 small pink hearts
    5 medium red hearts
    10 medium pink hearts
    8 large red hearts
    50 small peach jelly slices
    32 small candy bananas
    9 orange pinwheel hard candies
    9-ounce bag Nestlé's Merry Morsels
    8 red and white peppermint pinwheels
    8 red cinnamon buttons
container for tree stand — 10 inches wide and 5
    inches deep

Many of the candies listed can be found in bulk candy stores. If you cannot find the exact candies listed, try to find ones with similar shapes.

To make the cone that you will attach the candies to, take a piece of string about 20 inches long and tie one end to a pushpin and the other end to a pencil tied just above the point. The distance from the tip of the pin to the tip of the pencil should measure 18 inches. Insert the pushpin in the top center of the 28-inch square of foamcore. Keeping the string taut, draw an arc whose endpoints are 27 inches apart (fig. 1). Draw pencil lines with the ruler connecting the ends of the arc to the pinpoint. Next, divide the arc into 10 seg-

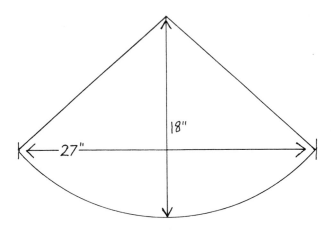

Figure 1

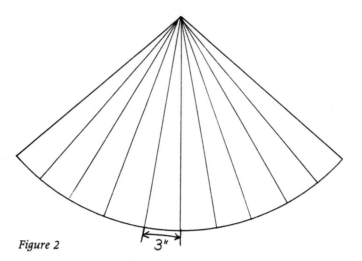

Figure 2   3"

ments of straight lines, each 3 inches wide. Use a ruler and draw lines with a pencil connecting the 3-inch points on the outer arc to the center pinpoint (fig. 2). With the X-acto knife and ruler, trim the outer curve from each segment so you are left with straight edges. This will be the bottom of the tree. Cut out the 2 lines connecting the ends of the arc to the pinpoint.

Next, score each segment along the pencil lines with the X-acto knife and the ruler, being sure to cut only halfway through the foamcore. Then bend all the segments in the same direction to form a cone. With white glue and masking tape, tape the two ends of the cone together along the inside seam. Generously glue the outside of the seam and tape over it. Let the cone dry on its side overnight, with the seam facing up.

Cut a hole in the center of the 10-inch foamcore circle, to the exact diameter of the cardboard tube. When the cone is dry, glue the bottom of the cone onto the circle. When this is dry, apply glue to one end of the cardboard tube and insert it through the hole in the circle, all the way to the top. Add glue around the tube where it meets the circle and then leave it upside down to dry, about 2 hours.

Using royal icing and the #16 tip, pipe a line of icing 8 inches down the cardboard tube, starting from where the tube meets the cone. Attach a candy stick along the line of icing. Continue adding icing and candy sticks around the tube until it is completely covered. Let it dry overnight.

To decorate the tree, first stand it upright between two stacks of books so that the tree is sitting on the books and the tube is hanging down between the two stacks. Start at the bottom of the cone, gluing spearmint leaves with a dot of royal icing on the back of each candy. Use the #3 tip on your pastry bag. Use the photograph as a guide, fitting the candies in between each other. Continue adding candies until the cone is covered.

When you have finished the tree, pipe a zigzag border of royal icing at the bottom with the #16 tip. Let it dry overnight.

To make a stand for the tree, take a container that is at least 10 inches wide and 5 inches deep and fill it about halfway with granulated sugar. Place the tube of the tree in the sugar, pushing it all the way to the bottom. Fill in the container with more sugar, leaving about 1½ inches to the top. Fill the top with assorted candies.

Chocolate Ornaments in a Chocolate Bowl

THIS EDIBLE centerpiece — a decorative ceramic-like bowl filled with Christmas ornaments — is made entirely of chocolate. It adds a touch of whimsy as well as beauty to the table, and it's so simple to make. Chocolate molds can be made in practically any type of container with a smooth surface.

Yields 1 bowl and 20 ornaments

1 pound each of white, milk, and dark coating chocolate
parchment-paper triangles
10-inch metal bowl
pastry brush
2 halves of a 2¾-inch plastic ball mold (found in cake-decorating stores)
small paintbrush

For piping chocolate, I prefer to use a cone made from a parchment triangle rather than a pastry bag. Parchment cones are disposable, so when the chocolate cools and becomes hard, you do not have to bother trying to get the chocolate out; you simply throw the cone away. You also do not fill a parchment cone as full as you would a reusable bag, so there is little waste.

To make a parchment cone, you can either buy ready-made triangles at a cake-decorating or cooking supply store, or you can make your own from a roll of parchment, found in the grocery store. To make a cone, hold the triangle so that the long side is facing up (fig. 1). Roll point A over to line up with point D and hold the two points together (fig. 2). Then roll point C to point D, making point B the tip of the cone (fig. 3). Adjust the tip of the cone until it is tight, leaving only a very tiny hole. I find it easier to handle if I staple the bag together at the top, thus preventing the bag from opening up while I'm working. Cut a small hole at the end of the cone, remembering that the chocolate will be runny and that the larger the hole, the faster and thicker the chocolate flow will be. Start with a smaller hole than you think you will need until you get used to piping in chocolate. Fill the bag with a few tablespoons of chocolate, fold the top in at the corners, then roll the bag down (fig. 4).

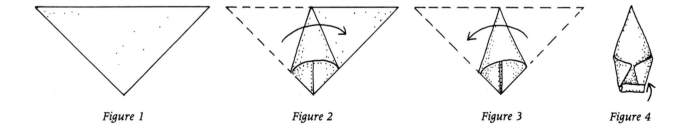

Figure 1   Figure 2   Figure 3   Figure 4

I use coating chocolate because it does not have to be tempered, making it much easier to work with. Also, coating chocolate does not have to be refrigerated, so you can leave your creations out for a long time. To melt the coating chocolate, place ½ pound of each of the 3 kinds of coating in 3 metal or glass bowls. You can add more chocolate to each bowl while you are working. Place each bowl over hot (not boiling) water and stir occasionally. To melt in the microwave, heat on low for 3 minutes and stir. Continue heating and stirring at 5-second intervals until the chocolate is completely melted.

To make the chocolate bowl, you will need 2 parchment cones. Fill one with melted white chocolate and pipe the design shown in pattern 1 on

Pattern 1

the inside of the 10-inch metal bowl. Fill the other cone with milk chocolate and pipe dots. Refrigerate the bowl for about 5 minutes, until the chocolate is hard. With the pastry brush, paint the inside of the bowl with dark chocolate. Begin by painting a thin layer of the chocolate on the bowl, then refrigerate for 5 minutes until it hardens. Then paint another layer. Continue until the chocolate is about ¼ inch thick. Refrigerate until all of the chocolate is hard and cold to the touch, then carefully pull the chocolate out of the bowl. If the chocolate is thick enough and completely cool, the bowl will not break. Try not to handle the shiny side of the bowl too much, as your fingers will leave marks on the surface.

To make the ornaments, pipe the chocolate on the inside of the ball halves. Make dots, spirals, stripes, or a filigree pattern (fig. 5). Chill the choc-

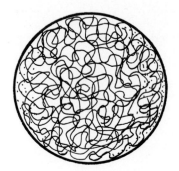

Figure 5

olate for a few minutes before adding a second color. You can then brush on or pipe a background color, making the chocolate no less than ⅛ inch thick. Refrigerate until the chocolate is cold. Pop the chocolate out of the mold. Pipe a little chocolate on the edge of the chocolate pieces and press the 2 halves together.

The Botanical Garden

THIS VICTORIAN-STYLE GREENHOUSE was inspired by the grand Enid A. Haupt Conservatory in the New York Botanical Garden in the Bronx. Made entirely of piped royal icing, the domed structure is built around the Christmas trees inside. You will amaze your friends — and yourself — when you finish this picturesque centerpiece.

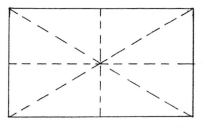

Figure 1

2 pieces of foamcore, 15¼ × 9 and 14¾ × 8½ inches
ruler
compass
X-acto knife
white glue
3 recipes royal icing, made with egg whites (page 145)
moss-green paste food coloring
pastry bags and couplers
tips #1, #2, #3, #15, and #18
3 ice cream cones
cookie sheets
wax paper
metal bowl, 9¾ inches wide at the top and 3½ inches deep
waterproof felt-tip pen
tape measure
vegetable shortening
Styrofoam ball, 4 inches in diameter
plastic wrap
small Styrofoam cone (found at craft stores)
piece of foamcore, 4 × 3 inches

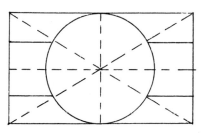

Figure 2

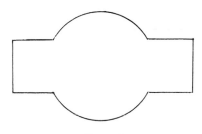

Figure 3

Start with the 2 foamcore boards to make the base. Find the center of each board by drawing an X connecting the 4 corners. Then divide each side in half and make a cross, connecting each of the center lines (fig. 1). On the larger board, draw a 9-inch circle with the compass, starting at the center of the crossed lines. On the other board, draw an 8½-inch circle (fig. 2). On the larger board, mark 2¼ inches above and below the center line on each short side; on the smaller board, mark 2 inches from the center lines (see fig. 2). Draw parallel lines from the marks on one short side to those on the other. Cut out with an X-acto knife up to the circle, then trim off the foamcore above and below on each board (fig. 3). Glue the smaller board in the center of the larger board.

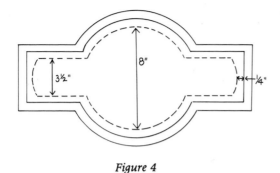

Figure 4

On the smaller board, draw the configuration shown (fig. 4). This will be your guide as to where to attach the icing pieces.

For this project, I recommend making the royal icing with egg whites rather than meringue powder because the icing will be stronger.

The 3 tallest trees are made on ice cream cones and the smaller ones are simply piped icing. The largest tree, in the center, should not exceed 5¾ inches high, and the two on either side should not exceed 4 inches. Make 1 recipe of royal icing, tint it green, and spoon it into a pastry bag fitted with the #18 tip. Glue the tallest cone to the center of the board with a little icing, then pipe branches, starting at the bottom of the cone and working your way up. Hold the tip at a right angle to the cone while applying pressure to the bag. Pipe a

star, then slowly pull the bag away from the cone, bringing the icing to a point. Place the next 2 cones on either side of the center tree, making sure that the trees are within the circle drawn on the board. Carefully break off a bit of the open edges of the cones to make them smaller than the tallest tree. Pipe branches on these 2 trees. To fill in the rest of the space with trees, pipe mounds of icing in spirals that come to a point at the top. Do not place any trees on the pencil lines (fig. 5).

Using a second recipe of royal icing, pipe the 16 arched windows (pattern 1). It is a good idea to make 20 copies of the pattern so that you can make all of the windows at once, with a few extras in case of breakage. Place the pattern on a cookie sheet and tape wax paper over it. Use the #2 tip to outline the windows and the #1 tip to pipe the windowpanes. Using the #2 tip, fill in the outlined outer area shown with thinned icing. Let dry overnight.

Cover a sheet of wax paper with a light coating of shortening. Pipe all of the side windows and roof pieces on the wax paper as marked on patterns 2–5. Let dry overnight.

To make the large dome, you will need a metal bowl 3½ inches deep and 9¾ inches wide at the top. This is a standard-size bowl found in cooking supply stores. The bowl should have a flat bottom

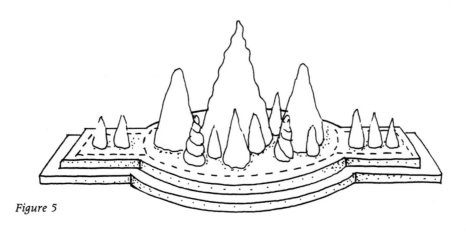

Figure 5

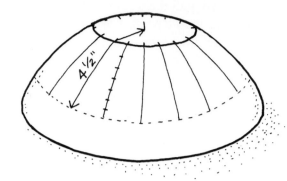

Figure 6

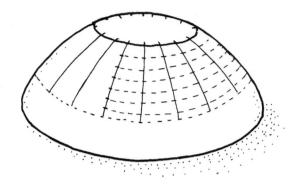

Figure 7

measuring 3½ inches across. Using a compass, draw a 3½-inch circle on a piece of paper. Cut out the circle and fold it in half, then into quarters, then eighths, then sixteenths. Open the circle and center it on the flat bottom of the bowl. Using a waterproof felt-tip pen, outline the circle on the bowl, then make a mark on the bowl at each of the 16 folds on the circle and another mark for the center of the circle. Place the end of a tape measure at the center of the circle and mark the bowl 4½ inches down, through one of the 16 marks. Draw a line with the marker along the tape measure, starting at the drawn circle, and mark off every ½ inch along the line (fig. 6). Mark all 16

lines this way. Next, connect all of the horizontal markings along the 16 lines (fig. 7). Save the paper circle for later.

Before piping on the bowl, you must coat it lightly with shortening, or the icing will stick to the bowl. Pipe double lines with the #3 tip along each of the 16 vertical lines (fig. 8). With the #2 tip, pipe horizontal lines at each of the marks along the vertical line (fig. 9). Next, pipe 2 evenly spaced vertical lines between each set of double lines (fig. 10). Then overpipe a third line between each double line. Let this dry overnight.

To make the smaller dome, cut off the top of a Styrofoam ball so that it is 1 inch high and 3½

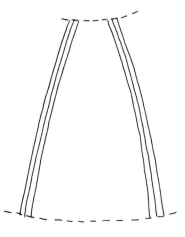

Figure 8

Figure 9

Figure 10

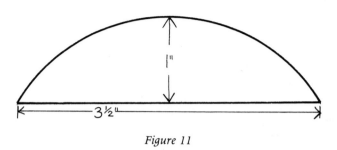

Figure 11

dome, with no creases, and tape it to the bottom. Cover the plastic lightly with shortening. Pipe double vertical lines on the dome with the #2 tip, in the same manner as on the larger dome. Pipe 3 horizontal lines, then 1 vertical line between each set of double lines. Finally, pipe another vertical line over the double lines (fig. 12). Let dry overnight.

To make the smallest dome, use the top of a Styrofoam cone, which should measure 1 inch wide and ½ inch high (fig. 13). Do not cut off the

inches across (fig. 11). (Use the larger half of the ball to sand the other piece to the correct size.) Tape the paper circle that you used for the metal bowl onto a larger piece of paper. Extend each of the 16 marks at the folds about ¼ inch onto the larger piece of paper. Mark the center top of the styrofoam dome with the marker. Place the Styrofoam dome in the center of the paper circle and mark each of the 16 divisions on the bottom edge of the dome. Draw lines on the dome from these marks to the center point. Make ¼-inch divisions on each line and connect these lines horizontally.

Cut a piece of plastic wrap a little larger than the dome. Wrap it tightly around the top of the

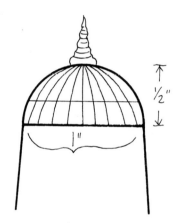

Figure 13

top of the cone. Cover the top of the cone with plastic wrap, taping it tightly around the cone. Cover the plastic with a thin coat of shortening. Pipe many vertical lines with the #1 tip from the center of the top of the dome, down ½ inch. Pipe a horizontal line around the center of the dome and one connecting the bottoms of all of the lines (see fig. 13). Pipe a cone on the top of the dome. Let this dry overnight.

To construct the building, start with the arched window pieces (pattern 1). Using icing piped from the #2 tip, attach the first piece to the board in the front center of the circle on the pencil outline. Hold the first piece in place while you pipe more

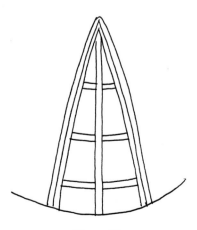

Figure 12

icing along one of its sides and on the board next to it. Place a second window next to the first one, pressing it into the wet icing. Place all of the windows around the circle in this way. Let them dry for a few hours before adding the domed roof pieces.

Next, attach the side panels (patterns 4 and 5) in the same manner as the arched windows, using the pencil lines as a guide. The longer pieces form the sides of the extensions, while the shorter pieces are joined to make the curved ends. Let these dry for a few hours before adding the roof pieces.

To make the domed roof, pipe a line of icing with the #3 tip along the top edge of the circle of arched windows. Carefully remove the large dome from the bowl, gently nudging the bottom of the dome to loosen it. Lift off the dome and place it carefully in the wet icing so that it is centered on the tops of the windows. Pipe a thin line of icing

around the base of the dome to help hold it in place. Let it dry for a few hours.

Meanwhile, add the roof to the side extensions. First attach one of the V-shaped pieces (pattern 2) to the top of the side extensions with a dot of icing on each side of the wall and on the top of the V, placing the top of the V against the arched window. There are 6 V-shaped pieces, which will be spaced evenly on the top of the extensions. You will have to hold each of the roof pieces for a short while until the icing sets. Try not to rush this step. Then add the 5 half-V roof pieces (pattern 3) to the top of the curved end of the wall. These will all meet at one point at the tip of the roof (fig. 14). When all of the roof pieces are in place, pipe a star border with the #15 tip around the bottom edge of the roof pieces, where the roof meets the sides. Pipe 2 evenly spaced horizontal lines across the roof with the #2 tip. Pipe a shell border with the #15 tip across the top center line of the roof.

Pattern 1
Bottom Windows, Make 16

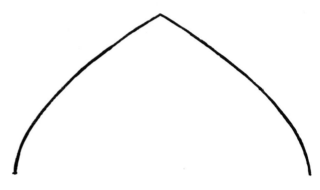

Pattern 2
Side Roof Pieces, Make 12

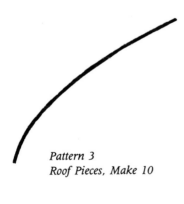

Pattern 3
Roof Pieces, Make 10

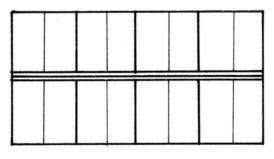

Pattern 4
Side Windows, Make 4

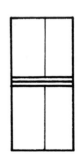

Pattern 5
End Windows, Make 10

To add the second dome, first cut 3 strips of foamcore 4 inches long by ¾ inch wide. Glue the strips on top of each other, which will make a strip about ¾ inch thick. Center this carefully on top of the large dome, making sure that it is steady. Carefully remove the smaller dome from the Styrofoam ball, gently pulling the plastic away from the icing. Center the smaller dome over the larger dome, setting it on the foamcore strip. Using the #2 tip, pipe vertical lines ³⁄₁₆ inch apart from the bottom of the smaller dome to the top of the larger dome, leaving gaps where the foamcore strip extends out (fig. 15). To pipe these lines (also called strings), attach the icing from the decorating tip to the bottom edge of the small dome and apply pressure to the bag. As the icing flows from the bag, move the bag down and attach the icing to the top edge of the large dome. If a string breaks while you are working, take a toothpick and re-

Figure 15

move the broken string, trying not to disturb any other strings. Let this dry for a few hours, then carefully pull out the foamcore strip. The smaller dome will be held up by the icing lines. Pipe lines to fill in the gaps left by the strip.

Attach the smallest dome in the same manner as the one below it.

When all of the pieces are in place, place the entire structure on a piece of wax paper that is larger than the base. Pipe a shell border with the #18 tip around the bottom edge of the base, around the edge of the second base, and around the bottom edge of the large dome. Pipe a smaller shell border with the #15 tip around the top edge of the large dome. Pipe dot borders with the #3 tip around the entire bottom edge of the building, up the divisions between the arched windows, and around the base of the small domes. Pipe a dot garland above each of the arched windows with the #2 tip, and a dot at each intersection of the garlands.

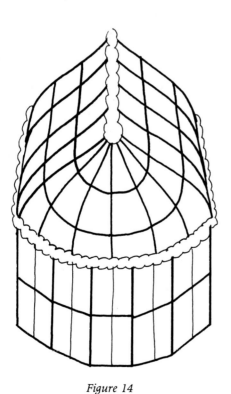

Figure 14

Basic Recipes

Basic Buttercream Icing

A VERY EASY buttercream that is good for both icing a cake and piping decorations and borders. It will stay fresh covered for 2 days without refrigeration, and can be stored in the refrigerator for 1 week.

Yields 6 cups

1 cup (2 sticks) butter or margarine, at room temperature (use vegetable shortening when pure white icing is needed)
½ cup milk, at room temperature
2 teaspoons vanilla extract or other desired flavoring
2 pounds confectioners' sugar

Combine all ingredients in large mixing bowl and mix at low speed until smooth. If stiffer icing is needed or the weather is very warm, add a little extra sugar. This recipe makes enough to cover and decorate a 9 × 13–inch sheet cake or 2 9-inch layers.

Meringue Buttercream

THIS IS a deliciously light and fluffy icing that is perfect for covering and filling a cake. It has a lighter taste than basic buttercream but is somewhat more complicated to make. It is not recommended in very hot and humid weather.

Yields 4½ cups

2 cups (4 sticks) unsalted butter, softened but cool
¼ cup water
1 cup granulated sugar
candy thermometer
5 large egg whites, at room temperature
½ teaspoon cream of tartar
glass measuring cup
2 teaspoons flavoring or liqueur

Beat the butter until smooth and set aside. In a small saucepan, combine the water and ¾ cup of sugar. Stir until the sugar is dissolved. Slowly heat the mixture, stirring constantly, until it starts to bubble. Reduce heat to low and insert a candy thermometer. Do not continue to stir.

In the large bowl of an electric mixer, beat the egg whites at medium speed until foamy. Add cream of tartar and beat at high speed until soft peaks form. Gradually add the remaining ¼ cup of sugar and beat until stiff peaks form.

Meanwhile, boil the sugar mixture until it reaches 248–250 degrees F on the candy thermometer. *Do not let the temperature go above 250 degrees F.* Turn off the heat and immediately pour the mixture into a glass measuring cup to stop the sugar from cooking. Pour a little of the sugar mixture onto the egg whites and beat them on low. Slowly add the rest of the sugar and then beat on high for 2 minutes. Beat on low until the mixture is cool.

Add the butter, 1 tablespoon at a time, to the egg-white mixture, beating continuously on low

until all of the butter is added. If the mixture starts to separate, beat on high for a few seconds until it solidifies. Beat until smooth, then add the flavoring. This icing can be stored at room temperature for 2 days or refrigerated for 10 days. This is enough icing to fill and cover a 2-layer 9-inch cake.

Royal Icing

ROYAL ICING is very versatile. It is pure white and dries very hard, so it is perfect for making flowers and bows and delicate piped work. It can be kept in an airtight container at room temperature for 2 weeks. You should stir the icing to restore its original consistency after storage, but do not rebeat. Royal icing does not work well in high humidity.

Yields 2½ cups

5 tablespoons meringue powder (found in cake-decorating stores)
½ cup minus 2 tablespoons water
   OR
2 egg whites, at room temperature
½ teaspoon cream of tartar
2 teaspoons water

1 pound confectioners' sugar

Place all of the ingredients in the bowl of an electric mixer and beat slowly until they are blended. Then beat at medium speed until the icing forms stiff peaks, about 5 minutes. Add more sugar if the icing is not stiff enough, or a few drops of water if it is too stiff. Use immediately or cover the bowl with a damp cloth to prevent drying when not in use. Allow at least 24 hours for royal-icing decorations to dry at room temperature.

Rolled Fondant

ROLLED FONDANT is a tasty, smooth icing that is rolled out with a rolling pin, draped over the cake, and smoothed down with the hands. Used mostly in England until recently, it has now become very popular in the United States. Fondant gives a cake a beautiful porcelainlike surface on which to decorate. Pre-made fondant can be purchased from cake-decorating suppliers and works very well.

Yields enough icing to cover a 9-inch cake, 4 inches high

2 pounds confectioners' sugar, sifted
¼ cup cold water
1 tablespoon unflavored gelatin
½ cup glucose (found in cake-decorating stores) or white corn syrup
1½ tablespoons glycerine (found in cake-decorating stores)
1 teaspoon desired flavoring (vanilla will give the fondant an off-white color)

In a large bowl (do not use metal), sift confectioners' sugar and make a well in the center. Pour water into a small saucepan and sprinkle gelatin on top to soften for about 5 minutes. Begin to heat the gelatin and stir until the gelatin is dissolved and clear. *Do not boil.* Turn off the heat and add the glucose and glycerine, stirring until well blended. Add the flavoring. Pour into the well of sugar and mix until all of the sugar is blended. Knead the icing with your hands until it becomes stiff and smooth. Add small amounts of confectioners' sugar if the mixture is sticky.

Shape the mixture into a ball, wrap it tightly in plastic wrap, and place it in an airtight container. This icing works best if allowed to rest at room temperature for about 8 hours, particularly if the weather is humid. Do not refrigerate fondant.

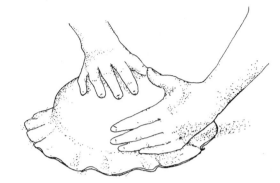

Figure 1

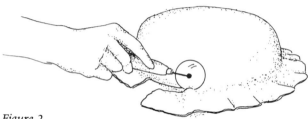

Figure 2

To cover a cake with fondant:

Dust a clean, smooth surface with cornstarch to prevent the fondant from sticking, and roll the fondant with a rolling pin until it is approximately ¼ inch thick. Make sure that the fondant is large enough to fit over the top and sides of the cake. Slide both hands under the fondant and carefully center it on top of a cake that has been freshly iced with buttercream. The icing makes the fondant adhere to the cake.

Dust your hands with cornstarch and smooth the fondant over the cake, starting at the top and working down the sides until the entire surface is even and flat (fig. 1). Cut off the excess fondant around the bottom of the cake with a pizza cutter or a sharp knife (fig. 2). Decorate the cake with buttercream or royal icing. The fondant keeps the cake fresh for 2 days at room temperature. Do not refrigerate a cake with rolled fondant icing.

Gum Paste

GUM PASTE is a very versatile *and edible* modeling material that is perfect for making realistic flowers, leaves, fruit, bows, and many other types of ornaments. It can be rolled very thin and dries very hard, almost like porcelain. It can be tinted with paste food coloring or brushed with edible powdered colors for a special effect.

1 cup Country Kitchen gum-paste mix (available in cake-decorating stores)
plus 1 tablespoon hot water (makes 5 ounces)
   OR
Bakel's Ready-to-Use gum paste
1 teaspoon gum tragacanth per pound of paste (found in cake-decorating stores)

Make the gum paste from the mix as directed on the package. Form it into a ball and rub it with a little vegetable shortening. Place it in a plastic bag and press out all of the air. Place the bag in an airtight container for at least 24 hours at room temperature. This gives the paste time to set. It will keep at room temperature for 4 weeks but should be kneaded occasionally to restore its elasticity. If longer storage is necessary, you can refrigerate the paste for up to 3 additional weeks. (Allow the gum paste to return to room temperature before using it.)

Always knead the paste before use. To test that it has the proper consistency, pull the paste apart; you should hear it "snap." If it does not snap, knead in some of the dry gum-paste mixture or powdered sugar until it reaches the proper consistency. If it is too dry or crumbly, knead in some shortening.

Colette's Chocolate Cake

THIS DELICIOUSLY rich cake is moist and very easy to make. It's my most popular cake.

Makes 2 9-inch layers, 2 inches high

2 cups sugar
1 cup unsweetened cocoa
1 cup vegetable shortening
1 teaspoon salt
2 teaspoons baking powder
1 teaspoon baking soda
3 cups sifted all-purpose flour
2 eggs, at room temperature
1 cup milk, at room temperature
1 teaspoon almond extract
1 teaspoon vanilla extract
1 cup hot, strong coffee

Preheat the oven to 350 degrees F. Grease the sides and bottom of the cake pans with shortening and then dust them with flour. In a large mixing bowl, combine all of the ingredients except the coffee. Mix at low speed until blended, scraping the sides of the bowl occasionally with a rubber spatula. Slowly add the coffee while mixing on low. Mix until smooth. Bake for about 30 minutes or until a toothpick inserted in the center comes out clean. Cool in the pans on wire racks for about 20 minutes, then invert onto racks and remove pans. Cool completely.

Gingerbread-House Dough

THIS is a perfect dough for constructing buildings and making ornaments, but it is a bit too hard for cookies.

½ cup firmly packed brown sugar
½ cup vegetable shortening
1 cup corn syrup (light or dark)
4 cups all-purpose flour
2½ teaspoons ground ginger
1½ teaspoons cinnamon
½ teaspoon salt
½ teaspoon nutmeg
¼ teaspoon allspice

Preheat the oven to 350 degrees F. Place the brown sugar, shortening, and corn syrup in a saucepan and heat on medium, stirring constantly until the shortening is melted. Place all of the dry ingredients in a large bowl, then add the warm sugar mixture, stirring until all the ingredients are well blended. The dough will appear crumbly but will hold together when rolled out.

Use the dough immediately, while it is still warm. If it starts to crumble, place it in a warm oven for a minute or two until it softens a bit. Bake on foil-lined cookie sheets for 10 to 15 minutes, depending on the size of the pattern (smaller pieces will take less time than larger ones).

General
Instructions
and Techniques

Glossary of Basic Tools

ALUMINUM FOIL: A useful item for many baking purposes.

CHOCOLATE COATING: Also called summer coating. Comes in dark, milk, white, and a variety of colors. Used for decorating when real chocolate is not required. Found in cake- and candy-supply stores.

CLOTH-COVERED WIRES: Found in florist's shops and cake-decorating stores, these come in white or green and in a variety of lengths and thicknesses.

COLUMNS: Plastic columns made specifically for cake decorating come in different heights and are designed to fit tightly into a top and bottom separator plate, which adds strength to the structure of the cake.

COMPASS: A simple metal tool that holds a pencil or lead and draws circles.

COUPLERS: Plastic couplers fit inside the pastry bag, and the decorating tip fits on top. The tip is then secured in place with a threaded ring. Couplers allow easy tip changing without the need to change bags. All decorating tips except for the very small or very large fit onto the couplers.

CUTTERS: Gum-paste cutters are specifically designed for making a variety of flowers in gum paste and can be purchased at cake-decorating stores, as can cookie and biscuit cutters.

DECORATING TIPS: There are hundreds of tips to choose from, but to start decorating, you can buy a beginner set of various tips and then buy other tips as needed. I find that I use the small round tips more than any others.

DECORATIVE FOIL: Found in cake-decorating stores, foil is used to cover cake boards.

DRAGÉES: These small and large silver- or gold-covered candy balls are nontoxic, but the Food and Drug Administration recommends that they be used for decoration only. They add sparkle to cakes, cookies, and ornaments. At this writing they are unavailable in California.

EDIBLE GLITTER: Glitter can be found at cake-decorating supply stores and comes in a variety of colors.

FLORIST'S TAPE: Florist's tape is used to cover wires and to bind multiple wired flowers and leaves together. It comes in white and green and can be found at flower shops and cake-decorating suppliers.

FLOWER NAILS: These flat or cupped supports on which flowers are piped can be found at cake-decorating stores.

FOAMCORE BOARD: Foamcore is a thin piece of styrofoam sandwiched between 2 pieces of thin white cardboard. I use this to make my cake bases and as supports between tiers. Foamcore is much stronger than and does not bend as easily as corrugated cardboard. It is easy to cut with an X-acto knife and can be used for many craft purposes.

FOOD COLORING: Food coloring comes in several forms: paste, liquid, and powder. The paste form is the most versatile. This is a highly concentrated coloring, and a little dab on the end of a toothpick is usually all you need. Paste food coloring can be found in cake-decorating supply stores. Liquid food colors, commonly found in grocery stores, can come in handy. However, to make the icing a dark color, you must add large amounts, which will thin the icing too much and make piping difficult. Powdered food colors are used for metallic and iridescent effects or for making very deep colors. Icing flowers can be dusted with powders and a small brush to give them a more realistic look. Powdered colors can also be made into a paint with the addition of a little bit of lemon extract, and applied with a paintbrush. At this writing, the Food and Drug Administration does not consider metallic powders edible, although they are nontoxic. They are to be used for decoration only.

HEAVY-DUTY MIXER: For the occasional baker, a regular upright mixer is fine, but if you are going to be doing a substantial amount of decorating, a heavy-duty mixer is best. Hand-held mixers tend to burn out and are not very efficient.

PAINTBRUSHES: Small, round, soft paintbrushes and pastry brushes come in handy for many decorating uses.

PASTRY BAGS: The best type of bag is the lightweight polyester kind. Cloth bags are bulky and hard to clean. Buy a few bags and keep the ones for royal icing separate from the ones for buttercream. The fat from the buttercream will break down royal icing, even if the bag is very thoroughly cleaned. I have found the 10-inch bag the easiest size to work with.

PIZZA CUTTER: This is a handy tool for trimming rolled fondant or for cutting strips of gum paste.

PLASTIC OR MARBLE CUTTING BOARD: Cutting boards are useful for rolling out gum paste. Plastic placemats can also be used and are less expensive.

PLASTIC WRAP: Has many uses for baking and decorating.

PRUNING SHEARS: These are used to trim dowels for tiered cakes.

ROLLING PIN: A large rolling pin is essential for rolling out fondant; small ones are better for rolling out gum paste.

RULER: An 18-inch metal ruler is the most versatile kind, but smaller rulers also come in handy.

SCISSORS: Large and small sharp scissors are a necessity for cutting paper, ribbons, and so on.

SEPARATOR PLATES: Plastic plates that come in a wide variety of sizes and are made specifically for cake-decorating purposes. Each plate has 4 pegs that are designed to snap into the tops and bottoms of plastic columns so that the top of the cake is secure.

SPATULA: Rubber spatulas are essential for scraping bowls of batter or icing. A stainless steel spatula is an absolute necessity. The one that I use the most is an 8-inch angled spatula. A plastic icing smoother is also a great aid when icing large cakes. These can be found in cake-decorating stores or in hardware stores in the spackling section.

TOOTHPICKS: Round toothpicks are useful for making stems for flowers and for adding paste colors to icing. They can also be used as a tool for embossing fondant or marking icing. Bamboo skewers can also be used when longer stems are needed.

TRACING WHEEL: Available in sewing stores, this inexpensive tool is good for embossing rolled fondant to give a quilted effect.

TURNTABLE: This is an invaluable tool that will make decorating much easier. You don't have to buy an expensive turntable; the plastic kind carried by most hardware stores (designed for storing spices) is fine and will support even the heaviest cake.

TWEEZERS: Tweezers are most helpful for picking up and positioning dragées or other small candies.

WAX PAPER: This is a must for the decorator or baker.

WOODEN DOWELS: Quarter-inch-thick wooden dowels can be bought at hardware or cake-decorating stores. They are used for supporting multiple-tiered cakes.

X-ACTO KNIFE: I constantly use an X-acto knife that has a long pointed (#11) blade. The knife has a thin metal handle and a blade that screws in and can be changed easily. You will need a lot of extra blades, since they tend to dull quickly.

Piping Techniques

THERE ARE many piping techniques used for decorating with icing. Once you have learned the basics, you can combine different techniques and even invent some of your own.

Lines

A common mistake many people make when piping straight and curved lines is to drag the tip and icing along the surface, which results in a wobbly, flat line. To make perfect clean and rounded lines, place the decorating tip against the surface on which you are piping and gently squeeze the bag. As the icing starts to flow out of the tip, lift the tip slightly up from the surface and move your hand with the bag along the line you wish to pipe. As the icing flows, it will settle on the surface in a nice clean line. Break off the icing when you reach the end.

Borders

Dot Border: Dots are made with a round tip. These vary in size, starting with the smallest tip, #00, and ranging up to #12. Depending on the size of the border desired, pick the appropriate-sized tip. Hold the tip perpendicular to the surface and apply pressure to the pastry bag. Squeeze until the dot is the size you wish. Slowly pull the tip away from the dot with a slight swirling motion so that the dot does not end in a point. Continue piping dots next to each other to form the border.

Shell Border: Shell borders are generally made with a star tip, #13 to #32. Other star tips are available, but these are the most commonly used. By using a round tip, you can make a faster version of the dot border. Simply hold the tip at a slight angle from your surface. While applying pressure to the bag, move the tip slightly to the left, then, as the icing starts to flow from the bag, move the tip up, apply more pressure to the pastry bag, and then move the tip down to the base and break off the icing, ending the shell in a point. Start the next shell on top of the end of the first one (fig. 1).

Star Border: The star border is made in the same way as the dot border. Hold the tip perpendicular to your surface and apply pressure. Pull the tip away when the desired-sized star is made (fig. 2).

Zigzags: A zigzag can be made with a star or a round tip. While applying pressure to the bag, move the tip up and down so that each line of icing is touching the one before it (fig. 3).

Figure 1

Figure 2

Figure 3

Run-in Sugar

RUN-IN SUGAR is a technique in which thinned royal icing is flooded into a pre-outlined shape on wax paper. When it dries, it is removed from the paper and applied to a cake for many decorative purposes.

The run-in sugar method can be used for making shapes on wires, toothpicks, or bamboo skewers, simply by laying a wire or skewer on the wax paper in the center of the design and outlining and filling in the design with the wire or skewer in place. The icing will dry with the wire or skewer tightly locked into the shape. You must also fill in the back of the design when the front has dried, to give the shape more strength. This also makes a design that can be seen from 2 sides.

To make run-in sugar designs, place the pattern you want to reproduce on a flat surface, such as a cookie sheet. Tape a piece of wax paper on top of the pattern. Outline the design on wax paper with stiff royal icing, using the #2 tip for small or intricate patterns or the #3 tip for larger designs. Place some stiff royal icing in a bowl and add a few drops of water while stirring. Continue adding water, a few drops at a time, until the icing has the consistency of corn syrup and a teaspoonful dropped into the bowl disappears by the count of

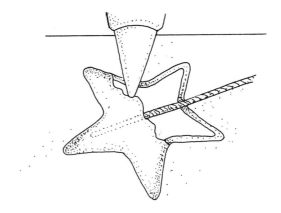

Figure 1

10. Pipe the run-in sugar into the outlined design with a #2 tip, filling in the entire shape up to the outline (fig. 1). Depending on the size of the design and the humidity in the air, allow at least 24 hours for the design to dry. Slide a metal spatula under the design to remove it from the wax paper. (*Hint:* When using 2 or more colors in a run-in design, allow the first color to dry before adding the second color. This will prevent the colors from bleeding into one another.)

Sugar Molds

MOLDING A FORM in sugar is an easy way to make edible ornaments. Any metal, plastic, or glass cup, bowl, or container can be used as your form for the mold. You probably have many containers in your home that will work quite well. The only thing to remember when looking for an appropriate container is that the top of the form should be wider than the bottom, or the sugar will not come out of the form. Sugar molds dry very hard and can be hollowed out before they are completely dry to make the mold more lightweight.

To make a sugar mold:

1 tablespoon cold water

1 cup granulated sugar (superfine sugar works best)

This recipe is enough to make a small mold, but if you are making something large, you will need to figure out how much sugar to use, keeping the same proportions as above. Since dry sugar takes up more space than wet sugar, first fill your chosen container 1½ times with dry sugar and pour it into a bowl. Measure the amount of sugar in the bowl, and this will tell you how much water is needed.

If you want to make a colored sugar mold, add some food coloring to the water before adding the water to the dry sugar.

Add the water to the sugar in a glass or plastic bowl. Mix by hand until all of the sugar is damp. Using your hand is messy, but it enables you to feel if the sugar is thoroughly mixed. Pack the sugar tightly into a clean container, pressing firmly with your hand. Level off the top with a knife and invert the container onto a piece of wax paper. Gently lift off the container. If the sugar doesn't come out easily, pick it up and turn it over again, tapping the container. Let the sugar mold set overnight, upside down.

After the mold has set, hollow it out by carefully turning the mold right side up and scooping out the still-damp sugar with a spoon. Be careful not to make the sides of the mold too thin, since the mold is not yet completely dry and could break. Then allow the mold to dry completely, right side up, for 24 hours.

Royal-Icing Bows

BOWS ARE a beautiful and festive addition to almost any cake, but they are especially great for holiday decorations. The tips listed will start you out with the basic technique, but you can use practically any tip to make the loops for a bow. Experiment with a number of different tips.

stiff royal icing, tinted to desired color (page 145)
pastry bag and coupler
tips #17, #48, #59 or #61, and #103 or #104
wax paper
metal spatula

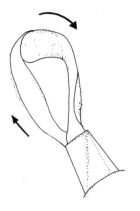

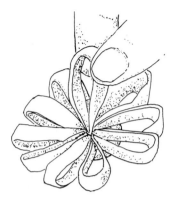

| Figure 1 | Figure 2 | Figure 3 |

Fill a pastry bag with royal icing and fit it with a tip. Place a sheet of wax paper on a cookie sheet. Hold the tip at a 45-degree angle against the paper. (If you are using a #59, #61, #103, or #104 tip, the wide end should be facing down.) Pipe a loop, keeping the tip upright and making sure that the loop ends in a point (fig. 1). Make about 25 loops. Let them dry for at least 8 hours.

To construct the bow, squeeze out a ring of stiff royal icing about 1 inch wide (or smaller for a small bow), the same color as the loops, using the #17 tip, either on the surface of a cake or on a piece of wax paper if the bow is to be applied

later. Place the pointed tips of the loops around the ring, in the wet icing (fig. 2). Pipe another ring of icing on top of the first one, a little closer to the center of the ring. Add another ring of loops on top of the first layer, placing the loops slightly upright. Add more icing to the center of the ring and finish the bow with the loops pointing upright (fig. 3).

If constructing the bow on wax paper, allow it to dry for at least 8 hours before attempting to remove it. Then carefully slide a metal spatula under the bow and set it with a dab of icing to hold it in place.

Gum-Paste Bows

gum paste
paste or powdered food coloring
small dish of vegetable shortening
plastic or marble cutting board
small plastic or wooden rolling pin
X-acto knife
ruler or measuring tape

small container of water
round toothpicks

Cover a cookie sheet with nontextured paper towels or facial tissue. This creates a surface on which the paste can dry without sticking.

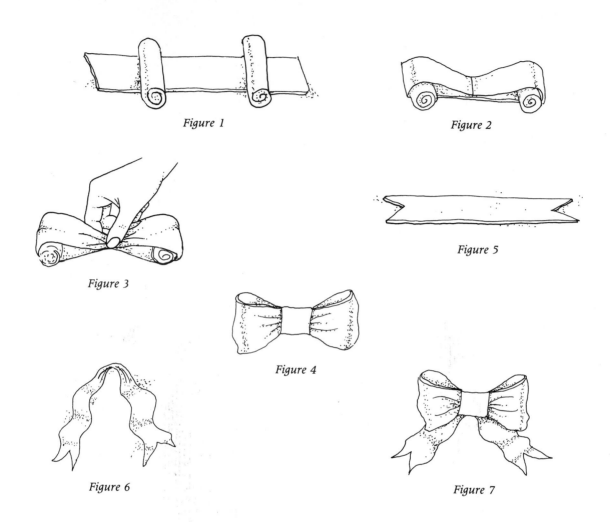

Figure 1

Figure 2

Figure 3

Figure 5

Figure 4

Figure 6

Figure 7

To make a knotted bow, tint the gum paste with paste coloring if desired and knead thoroughly. Rub a thin coating of vegetable shortening on a plastic or marble cutting board. Roll the paste as thin as possible, lifting and turning it after every roll. Do not turn the paste over. To make a small bow, cut strips with an X-acto knife ¾ inch wide and 5½ inches long. This is the proportion to use for all bows. Take 2 pieces of tissue and roll them into 2 tubes. Place them on the strip of gum paste, midway between the 2 halves of the strip (fig. 1). Dampen each end of the strip with a little water, then lift up each end and place it in the center of the strip, pressing it in place (fig. 2). The tissue will keep the paste from collapsing as it dries. Gently pinch together the center of the bow (fig. 3). Place the bow on the paper towel to dry.

After the bow has set for about 10 hours, add the center knot. Cut a strip of gum paste the same width as the original strip and just long enough to wrap around the center of the bow. Brush the back of the strip with a little water and wrap it around the center of the bow, placing the seam in the back (fig. 4). Let it dry for at least 24 more hours.

To make the ribbon ends for the bow, roll out the gum paste and cut a strip ¾ inch wide and 4½ inches long. Notch each end of the strip (fig. 5). Pinch together the center of the strip. Lay the strip on a piece of paper toweling, in a rippled formation, propping up the folds with pieces of tissue (fig. 6). Let the ribbon dry for 2 days.

To put together the knotted bow, place the center of the ribbon ends on a small mound of royal icing on the cake. Let this set for about 30 minutes. Place the bow on more icing in the center of the ribbon (fig. 7).

Cake Boards

WHEN creating a cake or fancy dessert, keep in mind that it needs to be placed on something. A crystal or silver platter can enhance an elegant confection, but one may not always be available. Presentation is important, and the choice of platter or board can either add to or detract from your labors.

I have found that a base made from foamcore board is quite versatile and can be easily cut to fit any design. You can cover the board with thinned royal icing or colored foil to contrast with or complement the cake or dessert.

When using foamcore as a cake base, you need to make sure that the board is thick enough to carry the weight of the cake. If the board is not thick enough, it will bend when lifted and the cake will crack. I have found that corrugated cardboard is not strong enough, because it tends to bend no matter how thick it is. Usually two layers of ¼-inch foamcore glued together will be strong enough to hold a single or two-tiered cake. The wider the base of the cake, the thicker the board should be. Glue the boards together with white glue and place some heavy books on top so they will dry flat.

To make a base from foamcore, trace the outline of the shape that you want on the board and cut it out with a sharp X-acto knife. The board should be at least 2 inches wider than the cake or dessert.

A simple way to cover the board is to use foil wrap that is specifically made for cake decorating. Foil wrap comes in a variety of colors and patterns and can be purchased at cake-decorating stores. Place the foamcore on the foil and cut out a piece that overlaps each side of the board by 2 inches. Wrap the foil around the board and tape it to the bottom using masking tape.

To cover a board with royal icing, glue the boards together to the desired thickness. Let the glue dry completely. Take enough icing to cover the board and thin it with water until the icing is the consistency of syrup. Tint the icing, if desired, and pour it onto the board. Smooth with a spatula and set aside to dry for 24 hours.

Since this method leaves the edge of the board uncovered, a ribbon should be glued around the perimeter. To place a ribbon on the edge of the board, spread a thin layer of glue on the edge, gluing a small amount at a time, and wrap the appropriate thickness of ribbon all around. This gives the cake a very elegant and professional look.

Whenever a cake is set on any kind of plate or board, a dab of icing is used to "glue" the cake in place. This prevents the cake from shifting. A dab of icing is also used to "glue" multiple tiers together. About a tablespoon of buttercream is enough to keep the cake in place.

Assembly of Tiered Cakes

THE CAKES in this book are made by placing one cake layer — the amount baked in one pan — on top of another, with filling in between. A tiered cake is made up of graduated layers. When making a cake with more than one tier, you have to reinforce the structure so that the weight of the layers does not make the bottom of the cake collapse. The structure is only as strong as its foundation. Additional support is provided by ¼-inch-wide wooden dowels inserted into the cake. Each tier is set on a separator board, which supports the cake on top of the dowels.

Each separator board should have the same circumference as the cake that it is supporting. Precut corrugated boards can be purchased in cake-decorating supply stores, but I prefer foamcore because it is both sturdy and lightweight. You can find foamcore in most art-supply stores, and it can be easily and cleanly cut with an X-acto knife.

To make separator boards for each tier, place the bottom of the pan in which your cake was baked on a piece of foamcore. Draw an outline around the pan and cut out the shape. This will give you a board the exact size of your tier.

When your cakes come out of the oven, they will usually not be perfectly flat on top. To make them level, wrap the cakes in plastic or foil and refrigerate them for a few hours, then unwrap them and cut off the tops horizontally with a serrated knife. It is easier to cut a chilled cake because there is less crumbling.

Next, place the cake on the foamcore. Spread a layer of filling on top, then add the second cake layer, top side down. This will give you a smooth, even surface on which to decorate. Fill in any gaps between the layers with icing.

To construct a three-tiered cake that has tiers 12 inches, 8 inches, and 6 inches in diameter, each tier being two layers thick, place the bottom layer of each cake on its corresponding separator board, using a dab of icing spread on the board to hold the cake in place. Spread filling on the bottom layer and add the top layer. Ice the top and sides of each tier.

Place the 12-inch tier on a cake plate or prepared board, using a dab of icing to hold it in place. When the icing on top is dry to the touch, place the bottom of the 8-inch pan on the center of the 12-inch tier. Lightly outline the pan with a toothpick. This will give you a perimeter within which to insert your dowels. Insert a dowel into the center of the 12-inch tier until it touches the board underneath. Clip the dowel with pruning shears level with the top of the cake. Insert six more dowels around the inside of the 8-inch circle and cut off the excess (fig. 1).

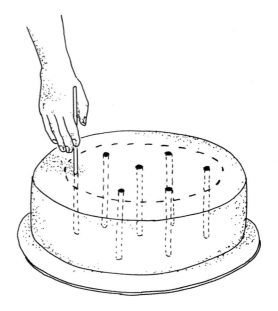

Figure 1

160

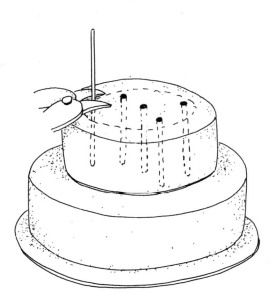

Figure 2

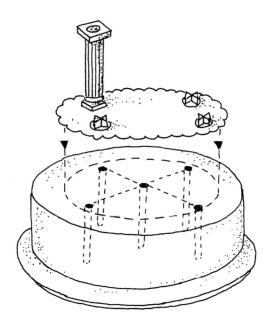

Figure 3

Spread a thin layer of icing on the bottom of the 12-inch tier to cover the dowels. Then place the 8-inch tier on its separator board on top of the 12-inch tier. Outline the 6-inch pan in the center of the 8-inch tier and insert dowels as before (fig. 2).

The top tier does not need any supports unless you are planning to place a heavy decoration on the top of the cake. In that case, you can insert three dowels in the top of the 6-inch tier.

If the bottom tier is larger than 12 inches, insert eight or nine dowels to give it added support.

When using plastic columns, use premade plastic separator plates instead of foamcore to support the columns. These plates have pegs on which the columns are placed. To support the plates, dowels are used in the same manner as above, except that these plates have indentations on the bottom to show you where to place your dowels. Press the plate gently into the top of the tier below and lift it off. Insert the dowels into the impressions left by the bottom of the plate (fig. 3).

Servings

THE TABLE below lists how many servings you can generally expect from various-sized and -shaped cakes, and the number of cake recipes you will need for each. Most cake recipes yield approximately 6 cups of batter, which will serve about 20 people. Each pan should be filled only halfway with batter to ensure maximum baking efficiency. Serving sizes will vary depending on who is cutting the cake, but the amounts given are based on pieces about 3 to 4 inches high and 1 to 2 inches wide.

Pan Size	Servings	Number of Cake Recipes Needed
6-inch round	10	½
8-inch round	20	1
9-inch round	25	1
10-inch round	35	1½
12-inch round	50	2
14-inch round	70	3
15-inch round	85	3½
16-inch round	100	4
6-inch square	15	¾
8-inch square	30	1
9-inch square	40	1½
10-inch square	50	2
12-inch square	70	3
14-inch square	100	4
16-inch square	125	5

Sources for Decorating Supplies

American Cake Decorating
A bimonthly magazine that features how-to's and reader contributions.
P.O. Box 1385
Sterling, Virginia 20167
703-430-2356
E-mail: addie@cakemag.com
Web site: www.cakemag.com

American Bakels
Ready-made rolled fondant in a variety of colors and flavors, and ready-made gum paste.
800-799-2253

Beryl's Cake Decorating Equipment
British bakeware and decorating supplies, by mail order only.
P.O. Box 1584
North Springfield, Virginia 22151
800-488-2749 or 703-256-6951
Fax: 703-750-3779
E-mail: beryls@internext.com

Colette's Cakes and Decorating School
681 Washington Street
New York, New York 10014
212-366-6530
Fax: 212-366-6003
E-mail: cakecolet@aol.com

CK Products
Wholesale and retail cake-decorating supplies.
310 Racquet Drive
Fort Wayne, Indiana 46825
219-484-2517
Fax: 219-484-2510

Creative Cutters
Gum-paste cutters and decorating supplies.
561 Edward Avenue #2
Richmond Hill, Ontario L4C 9W6
Canada
905-883-5638
Fax: 905-770-3091
For U.S. customers:
Tri-Main Building
2495 Main Street #433
Buffalo, New York 14214
888-805-3444

International Cake Exploration Society (ICES)
An organization of cake-decorating enthusiasts, which holds an annual convention in August.
318-746-2812
Fax: 318-746-4154
Web site: www.ices.org

International School of Confectionary Art
Classes in pulled sugar, chocolate, and cake decorating.
9209 Gaither Road
Gaithersburg, Maryland 20877
301-963-9077
Fax: 301-869-7669
E-mail: ESNotter@aol.com

New York Cake and Baking Distributor
Wide selection of products and equipment, available in-store and by mail order.
56 West 22nd Street
New York, New York 10010
800-94-CAKE-9 (942-2539) or 212-675-CAKE

Sugar Bouquets
Silicone molds and lace presses, mail order only.
800-203-0629 or 973-538-3542
Fax: 973-538-4939

Sunflower Sugar Arts
Metal gum-paste cutters, silicone mats and lace molds, veining and gum-paste tools, and powdered colors.
P.O. Box 780504
Maspeth, New York 11378
914-227-6342
Fax: 914-227-8306

Pearl Paint
Sellers of art supplies, including foamcore, Styrofoam, X-Acto knives.
308 Canal Street
New York, New York 10013
212-431-7932

Wilton Enterprises
Bakeware, decorating tools and supplies, and cake-decorating classes.
2240 West Seventy-fifth Street
Woodridge, Illinois 60517
800-942-8881
Web site: www.wilton.com

Index